THE EX-WIFE
Now What's *Next* ??

THE EX-WIFE
Now What's *Next* ??

by Ignatius J

*Don't confuse what God wanted you to go through
with what you decided to deal with*

Zigg @XaviercMiller

To the living:

Marilyn Lashell

Paula Andrea

Paul Ignatius

Minnie Lee

Doris Louise

Noah Sr.

and the transitioned:

Lilian Wright

Paul (Mickey) Hodges

Susie Roberson

Kevin Pain

Clara Danielle Wilkins-Jones

Jacob Williams

Edna (Dot) Holmes

Katherine Jones

TABLE OF CONTENTS

ACKNOWLEDGMENTS

My Higher Power, my God, the universe, my ancestors - I am forever grateful and humble. Thank you for the opportunity to grow and become the man that I am today.

Clara Marie, my sweet, precious mother. I'll miss you as long as I live. I will continue this earthly journey with my head up high and with you in my heart.

Lilian Wright, grandmother of my children. My second mother, if you will. I love you and miss you. Thank you for the love you've always shown me.

Paul (Mickey) Hodges, I was shocked to hear of your passing, my love. I am grateful for the time we shared.

Clara Danielle, my beautiful cousin. Thank you for the love you showed me.

Jacob Williams, your passing was a shock to me. I'll always remember you.

Edna (Dot), my loving auntie. I am grateful for the times we shared talking and watching old black and white tv shows.

Katherine Jones, I am saddened by your passing. I am glad I got to spend time with you before you transitioned.

DISCLAIMER

I would like to thank the real-life members of my family, friends, and acquaintances portrayed in this book for each individual life experience that we shared along this life journey. Be it good, bad, or ugly, it was an experience that taught me, shaped me, and made me. I am a firm believer that everything happens for a reason and everyone is in your life for a reason and season. This book contains diary and journal inserts that I have written over the course of 38 years and memories that I bore. I understand that my memories of the encounters with my family, friends, and acquaintances may differ from their recollections of the events described in this book. These accounts are not perfectly precise, but are to the best of my knowledge and from what I have written during the time of the events when the events occurred. I have changed the identities of those that are mentioned in this book to protect their identities and to stave off legal woes.

CHAPTER 1

Nobody's Supposed To Be Here

KEISHA -THE EX -WIFE

ow did you get here?

Two wolves in sheep's clothing. Keisha and I met at church around July 1998. At that time, I was deeply involved in church activities. I was in training to become a preacher, teaching Sunday school for the teenage youth group at the church and serving as the church bus driver. My Sundays were packed with three worship services, and I also attended Wednesday evening bible study and Thursday night preacher training class. I was always dressed in dress shirts, ties and slacks. Keisha was one of the church members that I picked up on my route to church. I thought she was very pretty, resembling Taraji P. Henson, with an innocent look about her. I would even say she was homely. Establishing anything more than a friendship was not on my mind. At the time, I was already talking to Shannon, a young lady from a sister congregation. Shannon was very pretty as well - a little on the heavy side, but she had a cool personality and an inviting demeanor. After a few conversations with Keisha, I realized she was feeling me, and I found myself returning those feelings. So,

I stopped talking to Shannon, then Keisha and I began getting to know one another.

Journal insert

04SEPT1998: What's up, yo? I know it's been a while since I last wrote but I will when I can. At this present time, I'm outside of Kinko's waiting for Keisha to finish faxing resumes. Keisha is a young lady I met at church. She was baptized a couple of weeks ago. Since I lost my car in May, I've been driving the church van. I pick up those in need of a ride. Keisha happened to be one of those in need of a ride because her car was stolen not too long ago. The first time I saw her, I noticed her but by her being a new church member, I wasn't going to approach her. I had been out with Shannon once and I thought something was going to transpire between us. I really was not that attracted to Shannon because she's slightly overweight. I'm not a shallow person. I just know what I'm attracted to. A young lady approached me, named Tiffany, as I was leaving the liquor store across the street from Smart and Final after I bought a beer. Yeah, I know, but that's a different story. I went by Tiffany's apartment to visit once, and she came by my apartment for a brief visit. I can tell she wants to get at me in more ways than one. I'm not going down that road again so that's on that. I'm more interested in Keisha because we both have the same dreams of being married. We want to date but we both want to get advice from Brother Cooper.

Journal insert

12SEPT1998: As you have noticed, I didn't get to finish. Right now, I'm at a religious debate at church. Brother Cooper is debating a Muslim young brother about Paul. Muslims believe that Paul is the anti-Christ. Anyway, since September 4th, I have talked to Brother Cooper about dating Keisha. He was happy to hear that Keisha was /is interested in me and not any other brother at the church. He told me that it is okay for us to kiss but to be careful not to take it any further. I know that I don't want to make the same mistakes I've made in the past. Last night, September 11th, she came over to my apartment. We cooked dinner and ate. We began to watch a movie. We started kissing and we fornicated. I repented of that, and it will not happen again until we're married. Keisha will soon become my wife. I hope and pray that it is in our Father's will!!!

"I's married now"! September 30, 1998. Keisha and I got married after only a few weeks of knowing one another. It definitely wasn't a love-at-first-sight thing. It was more like, *I'm 28, getting older, and I should settle down and get married.* I proposed to her at a restaurant whose name I can't even remember. We got our rings from a jewelry store in the mall.

I was reluctant and unsure about getting married so quickly, but I did it anyway. We went through with it because we wanted to be good "Christians". Abdul was my best man. My brother was there, salty because I didn't choose him to be my best man. In retaliation, he got married while I was stationed in Korea. Alan didn't t like Keisha anyway, and he made sure she knew it. He called her a hood rat all the time.

No one knew I was getting married— not my mother, not my daughters, and not even Destiny. When I told Renee, she was in disbelief and came over to my apartment to talk to me and find out what was really going on.

Journal insert

20OCT1998: Well, I know I haven't written in a while. Don't feel bad. There isn't anything I can think of that I do on a regular basis. I believe a few things have occurred since I last wrote. I've been married for almost a month now. Yes, I tied the knot on September 30th on Abdul and India's fourth wedding anniversary. Marriage is definitely not what I anticipated. Within this first month of our holy matrimony, we have argued several times. By the way, I married Keisha Marie. We got married at in San Bernardino. We both didn't want to continue to fornicate against God. We've both been through crappy relationships. We both believe in marriage and against divorce. At least I used to be against divorce; honestly the word has been on my mind lately. Simply because once again I have found a woman that doesn't respect me. She curses at me, she calls me names: STUPID, DUMB ASS NIGGA, and so on. Today she cursed in front of Tomia and that really PISSED me off!

Journal insert

26OCT1998: Keisha grabbed my journal and read it. I guess I will continue from where I left off. I guess this relationship isn't as mature as I would like it to be. Like I wrote in the letter to moms: Keisha and I have a lot of growing to do especially since we haven't known each other that long. As I was writing earlier in this journal, she doesn't respect me. If she did, she would not have taken my journal and shoved it down her pants because I told her she couldn't read it. I believe it has more to do with maturity and respect. (*Remember when you used to read ... nvm go ahead*). Just like today, she asked if she could have a hand mirror that she found while snooping in my box for my journal. I told her that it belongs to Tomia then she knocked it off the dresser. The more I write, the more I realize that it really is a maturity issue. I don't know how I'm going to handle this. Sister Turner, from church, had a meeting with Keisha and I last Tuesday evening over dinner at Home Town Buffet. It was beneficial, I think. We're supposed to meet with her once a week.

On to something else before my hand gets tired of writing. I don't know if I wrote that my Kia Sportage got repossessed on May 22, the day after I made a payment on it. It was still behind two more payments! So, I started driving the church van and picking up the church members. The van wasn't in the best of shape mechanically. While in my possession I was supposed to check the oil regularly, but I didn't. It eventually threw a rod and broke down on me. This happened about two months ago. Brother Cooper along with the church is trying to get a collection to get the van fixed. He made a few statements about it such as, "Those who require services of the van should basically give more." Not in those exact words but that's what he was getting at. Keisha asked me if I was going to drive the van once it's fixed. I told her, "No." I don't even plan on riding in it let alone drive it!!!

This church works my nerves in a bad way sometimes. I don't want anything from this church. ANYTHING!!! I'd rather do without. May God forgive me if I am wrong but that's the way I feel. I'm working at Pic n Save again and this time I'm really going to try and get it together. Keisha asked if she could budget our money. After being reluctant, I gave her the okay. All I have to provide the house with is $150 a week and the rest I do what I want. During this time of year, I should be able to pay off some of these monkeys on my back. Even though Keisha and I argue almost every day, I believe she is a help in my life. I'll write more later. I'm going to start finding time to write more each day and study my bible and catch up on things.

Journal insert

11NOV1998: What's the deally yo!? I'm on the bus waiting for the driver to finish her break. I just got off work from Pic n Save at 3:00 p.m. I've been working since 2:00 a.m. I had to be at Smart and Final at 2:00 a.m. I worked there until 10:00 a.m. eight hours. Then I had to be at Pic n Save at 11:00 a.m. I worked there until 3:00 p.m. 12 hours. Traveling home by bus. I see this as paying my dues! I'm really working towards getting another car. Between both jobs, my hours have been crazy, but I've been maintaining 40+ hours a week between both jobs.

Keisha and I took Tomia clothes shopping for school last Saturday. Keisha picked out most of the clothes. It really felt good working all those hours, then at the end of the week take Tomia shopping with my wife.

Journal insert

01JAN199: Well, I know it's been a while. I have been going through so much drama, it's crazy. I'm learning more and more not to try to predict what God has planned. Part of me believes that God placed Keisha in my life. But the way our relationship has been going, I feel confused. She has called the police on me twice. Both times because I wouldn't let her take the car. We got a car a couple of months ago. The first time she called the police, well right before she called, we were arguing because she wanted to leave, and I wouldn't give her the keys. I believe it was almost 11:00 p.m. She got mad and punched me in the stomach HARD!! I pushed her on the bed, and she called the police. I called Abdul and told him what happened. He told me the police were going to take me to jail so I ran out the apartment with no shoes or socks on. Like a runaway slave. She ran out of the door after me. I jumped the gate into the condo complex next door. I walked all the way to Allison's apartment.

By this time, it was close to 2:00 a.m. I woke Allison up and asked if I could just crash in the living room. She said it was okay. I called my apartment to see if Abdul had made it over there. After the first ring, I figured that Allison's number would show up on the caller ID so I hung up.

I finally got in touch with Abdul, and he came and picked me up and took me home. I slept in Tomia's room with my brother while silently crying and sobbing. Keisha was in our bedroom blasting the stereo. The next day, I didn't go to work. I stayed home with Keisha all day. I really don't know what is going to happen with us. That one incident was just one of many. Yeah, I know, what have I got myself into? Well, I know I'm not the Christian I used to be and that's where all this turmoil is coming from. I'm not in denial that there are definitely serious issues that we definitely have to work out; or go on about our business, DIVORCE. I know that I am not a believer of divorce and that there is only one reason for divorce that God will accept and that is if one of us have an affair. Well, that line has been crossed already.

Keisha screwed some chump name Miles that she was screwing before we got together. She screwed him on December 31st, 1998. That morning was a strike in our relationship. Not that she screwed him that morning because I didn't get her confession until a week later!!! That morning started off with us fucking. I came and she was on top of me, and I went limp. She continued to grind my limp dick. I suggested that she stroke it with her hand so it would get hard. She got upset, then I got pissed. Next, we exchanged a few negative words. I pushed her off me onto the floor. She got up and started swinging at me, so I grabbed her by her hair and pushed her face into the bed. I told her not to fuck with me. She got up and showered. After her shower, she told me she was going to the bank. That was on a Thursday. I came to find out that's when she went and fucked Miles.

Journal insert

APR 1999: I sit here in the car on a so-called gloomy Saturday evening listening to 98.3 F. M. radio station drinking an ice-cold

Old English beer. Just chillin alone while my wife and daughter await my presence. So much is going on in my life especially with my wife. I dare not complain because I have so much to be grateful for and I am!! It's just my wife. She challenges my every word, mocks my actions, and disturbs my inner soul! I know I shouldn't allow her to get to me, but she really does.

At this time in life, I've been working (I'm still at Smart and Final - six years in May) about 30 hours a week, attending a bible video at church (which I've been a member of since September 5, 1996) every Thursday 6 p.m. - 9 p.m. and Saturday 4 p.m. - 7 p.m., attending bible study on Wednesdays 7 p.m. - 8 p.m., and Sunday service twice on Sundays. I sometimes attend Sunday morning bible study before first service. Now, every now and then I hang out with Blue and Kirk and probably hang out at a club and have a few drinks, but I remain faithful! She still finds reasons to put me down, nag me, insult me, and disrespect me. Constantly complaining; never satisfied! I really don't know how much I'm going to tolerate. Unfortunately, Destiny has recently gone to jail. But fortunately, Tomia is with me and will be for a few weeks. **Patricia, Destiny's aunt, went up to Ross with Tomia, where Destiny was working. During this time, Destiny and Auntie Pat were heavily involved in boosting and shoplifting. While working, Destiny spotted an abandoned credit card sitting on the counter at a cash register. She called her aunt to come to Ross to retrieve said card.**

I can only assume that Aunt Pat began shopping, and when she used the credit card to purchase items, she and Destiny were apprehended. They were both handcuffed and

held in the back office with Tomia, awaiting the police. I had Destiny's car that day, so I went up to Ross to pick her up. When I arrived, the manager informed me that Destiny was being held in the back and that I could not see her, but I could take my daughter. **WHAT IN THE ENTIRE FUCK MAN?! I was conflicted, of course** — because of the whole situation and because even though we were not together when she boosted, she got shit for me as well. Destiny had a history of theft that dated back to our days at McDonald's, and maybe even before we met. I also had sticky fingers but never bold enough to shoplift.

After about a month or two in jail, she was given probation and assigned to Glen Helen, where she worked on the weekends to pay off her debt to society. Destiny violated her probation, and her next court date is May 13th. I've always felt that Tomia would be with me, but I never imagined (I don't think) how God would work that out. I really feel for Des because she's been working full time since September and seemed to have been doing great. But I must remember that she has been living in constant sin also. I'm going to wrap this up because I think I've been gone at least an hour or more. I started writing because I had an idea for a movie. I know my life experience makes a lot of movies a lot!!!! I just had an idea for another one.

Journal insert

28APR1999: I'm sitting in the car once again. Except this time, I'm waiting on Keisha to get off work. She gets off at 4:30 p.m. so I really don't' have much time to write. Today I went to work, still at Smart and Final on Baseline. Thank God! I went in at 5:00 a.m. and got off at 7:00 a.m. to go home to pick up Keisha and Tomia. Keisha called my job around 6:30 a.m. to ask me about some socks that Tomia should wear to school. I told her what she decided was fine and that I would be there to pick them up at 7:15 a.m. When I walked into the apartment, Tomia was about to sit down to eat a bowl of cereal. I told her it was time to go. She was upset. Before I left for work, I set the alarm clock for 6:00 a.m. I know she didn't get up because if she did, she would have had enough time to eat. Yesterday I ironed Tomia's clothes for school for today, so all Keisha had to do was wake Tomia up, fix her a bowl of cereal, and do her hair which was already in braids.

Journal insert

*30APR1999 – 4:*16 PM: At this present time, I am sitting in the car waiting for Keisha to get off work. Today I really don't have anything to complain about; thank you Jesus! I got going this morning about 6:16 a.m. I woke Tomia up and while she was in the bathroom washing up, I ironed her school clothes. After ironing Tomia's clothes, I ironed my clothes. I had to go to San Bernardino Valley College to do a speech today that I wasn't able to do last year for my finals because my car got reposed. Anyway, after I ironed my clothes, I ironed Keisha's clothes for work. I dropped Keisha off at work and got a little kiss. Then I dropped Tomia off at school and got another little kiss. I went to Destiny's apartment to pick up some more clothes for Tomia to wear to school.

As I entered the gate into the apartments, Lucas was leaving out. We waved at each other. Violet gave me Tomia's clothes. She really wasn't doing too well. She lost her job last week for being late all the time. I don't know when she dropped out of college. I have to pray about her and for her. I went back home to brush up on my speech then I went to school. I practiced for the last couple of days. There were only about ten other students that had to make up their speech also. I think I did the best out of the class because the instructor commented and complimented me a lot. I got a "B". I prayed on the way to school for confidence. On my evaluation the instructor wrote I displayed a lot of confidence. I felt good and I still do.

Journal insert

30APR1999: After I had gone upstairs that Saturday, Keisha and I got into an argument that led to us getting into a big fight in the car as I was taking her to her grandfather's house. She had been drinking also and things got ugly in the car on the freeway. She got upset and lost control of herself and threw her boom box out of the car window that was rolled up. So, after she broke the window, she started hitting me and punched me in the face. So I pulled the car on the side of the freeway after pushing her off of me. I got out of the car and proceeded to walk off the freeway. She put the car in reverse and told me to get in. I looked at her and continued to walk towards the freeway exit. She tried to run the car up the hill and hit me (I can't really say it was a serious attempt). I kept walking and she drove off.

I called Blue on my cellular phone and told him to pick me up at Ruby's BBQ. He picked me up and we talked about what happened. He took me to Mark's apartment where he lives. They had a few friends over watching the movie Belly on video tape. David was there, this one cat I had met before. There was another dude there, I think his name was Troy. He was a slim light skin red bone, really cute. I think he is either gay or bisexual. I'll probably find out in the future. I don't know if he lives there or if he just visits or if he is a friend of Mark's or Selma's (Mark's fiancé). I do know I would like to know him.

Anyway, I called Mickey to pick me up. I don't know if I wrote about Mickey before or not but anyhow, he's this dude I used to fuck around with a few years back. He came and picked me up looking cute. He's changed some, he smokes bud now and drinks. He took me to pick up Tomia from Barbara's apartment because I had her daughter watching her. (She didn't want to do it but it's okay). We took Tomia to her aunt Pat's house. Then, we went and got some condoms and lube and went to a hotel.

The first room we went into there was a couple already in there. They had snuck in. They asked us to give them a minute to leave. We just got another room. He asked me to undress in front of him, so I did. I pulled his pants down and sucked him until he almost came. He put the condom on, lubed up my chocolate ass hole, and proceeded to put himself inside me. I was really tight. I couldn't loosen up. Mickey started fucking me so hard and deep I could barely take it. He kept smacking my legs, a little too hard, then he came. I got up and showered or washed off. He did the same and then took me home. I know my life is a mess and I really don't expect anyone to understand because I don't quite understand it myself. I don't know where I'm headed, I just hope it's not hell!! I'm going to have to start seeing a counselor. Maybe that will help me come to some kind of conclusion about a definite direction, as far as career wise and sexuality. I know that I enjoy anal sex, maybe if I just bought Keisha some toys, I can be fulfilled that way. I wrote before that I know I'm not gay because I love pussy, but I also love dick. I'm attracted to women and find them sexually appealing, and I'm attracted to men and find them to be sexually appealing as well. There is just a difference in the attraction!! Is that my fault?!!

CHAPTER II

Sweet Sadie (Mahalia)

· ● ·

Tomia and I flew to New York in May 1999 to attend my granny's funeral. At the time, I didn't have any money to cover the trip. Major, my boss from Smart and Final, generously loaned me enough money not only my ticket but also for Tomia to come with me.

My uncle Ronnie had been living in New York for as long as I can remember. He had been taking care of Granny ever since she had moved in with him in 1997. My mom and Aunt Darlene moved to New York in 1998 to assist him in caring for her.

I later heard that the church was upset with me for taking Tomia instead of my wife. Looking back, maybe a more mature husband would have taken his wife, even if we were at odds. But at that time, I couldn't care less about what the church thought. When I went to them for help to go to New York for my granny's funeral, they only offered me a Greyhound bus ticket — just for me.

Journal insert

13MAY1999: At this present time in life, I'm 263 miles from California, hundreds of feet in the air and traveling at 613 miles per hour. You guessed it, I'm in an airplane. I'm on my way to New York. It's not quite a vacation but I am using some of my vacation time. I have to go because on Friday May 7th, my granny Mrs. Mahalia passed away at the age of 85. I don't care to hear people tell me she lived a full life! To me my granny was never really happy. Maybe because of my definition of happiness. I have to realize that everybody's definition of happiness is not the same! I just wish granny didn't have to leave so soon!

New York - well this will be my first time going to the big apple. I'm a little excited and I'm not really impressed! I know I can't really say that because I haven't gotten there yet. I guess because of the family situation I can't be totally excited. Friday the 7th after my mom called my job and told me the sad news about granny's death, I went and got her name tattooed on my right shoulder. I also went by Alan's job to pick him up and inform him of granny's passing. When I got to his job he was walking off. I got out of the car and approached him. He walked away from me and told me he already knew. I told him, "God bless you too." Then I left. I haven't talked to Alan since he moved out of my apartment late February 1999.

The only reason I tried to reach out to him Friday was because I didn't want him finding out about granny over the phone like I did and then catching the bus home. I tried to be there for him. I tried to humble myself. I really don't think that I'll try again!!!

Alan may feel that I've done him wrong after I asked him to move out after living with me since 1996. I got married. My so-called wife was stressing me because Alan and Evan, a brother from church, were living with us. I did what I thought was best. Ever since then I've made sure Alan got his mail that was delivered to my place. NOT ANYMORE!! I hope and pray that when I leave New York, I am a stronger person because I'm tired of other people's BULLSHIT!! I means THAT!! I'll be in New York for a week and a few days. Tomia is with me. Destiny just got out of jail about a week ago. She and I went out for drinks the other night. It was cool.

Journal insert

20MAY1999: Well, I'm just sitting here thinking. Mom is downstairs on the stoop with Tomia. I just remembered I have to go down to Uncle Ronnie's apartment so Tomia can call her mom. Destiny called out here yesterday, but Tomia was upstairs. I just want to write what's on my mind. I just lost my granny a couple of weeks ago and I just feel that my heart won't cry any more. I'm hurt and I'll forever miss her, but I guess she's in a better place, only God knows.

I'm not planning on going back to that same church anymore when I get back to California. I'm really tired of the bullshit there. I look at it like this, I'm a father working a part-time job and maybe I'm not trying my best, but I am trying! They could have helped me to get out here to be with my family without constantly telling me it would be a loan and not benevolence. I know it's because the church van engine broke down due to my neglect. I didn't check the engine, well the oil. The engine light has always been broken. Thanks to Keisha, half the church knows that I had an affair with a man. My sexuality is still a struggle for me. I know I have, well, I feel that I have to be strong and do what's right. The only thing that I feel would be right is to work things out with my wife. But will that make me happy?!!!

Journal insert

21MAY1999: I was just sitting here thinking after watching Ellen DeGeneres's television sitcom, *Ellen.* I'm tripping because I wrote against homosexuality in my speech for my finals at San Bernardino Valley College (SBVC). I wrote that sitcoms such as Ellen are not good. I just finished watching two episodes of the show. The second episode caught my attention and inspired me to write. Ellen's cousin had passed out from fumes and dreamed that homosexuals were the majority in the world and heterosexuals were the minority. My belief in the bible condemns me for my thoughts. Sodom and Gomorrah were destroyed because they were cities filled with homosexuals. Even though I don't consider myself to be homosexual, I feel that I am still damned because I burn so deeply inside to be with men and fornication is still considered a sin!

There's just no way around it or anyway to justify it! I realize that Jesus died for my sins and God is a just God and HE knows we all fall short of HIS glory. I just don't know what to do! Well, what really prompted me to write was the fact that I was thinking about all the things I like about men and what attracts me to them. As well as all the things I like about women and what attracts me to them. **Refer to** *Journal Insert: February 2, 1993,* **for detailed list**.

Journal insert

*30MAY1999:*I 'm so fuckin mad and frustrated right now. I just want to tear some shit up. I'm tired of dealing with Keisha fuckin ass first of all!!! I don't think I would have ever anticipated marriage would be like this! It's really beyond words but I'll try to explain. I know that I'm not perfect and I will never be. I smoke and drink and fuck around when I can; simply because Keisha fuckin never want to give me any pussy unless she's horny. True, in the beginning of this nightmare called marriage she wanted it more than I did but I was tired a lot!! Working two jobs and going to church wore me out. Her ass has no excuses. I didn't fuckin get married to be denied of sex!!! That's what got me caught up in this shit from the get-go!!! Now she's gone with the car, and I'm stuck in the fuckin house waiting on Renee to get back from Los Angeles. I'm supposed to go by DeAdrian house today because he's barbecuing. I went there last night for a little while with Kirk and Abdul. Abdul was acting an ass!!! Today when I talked to him, he told me his wife said that she is going to pay her cousin to jump me!! Can you believe that shit!!! His wife and Keisha don't like Abdul and I hanging out so much. His wife also asked him if he was gay with me!! I'm tired of this bullshit!!! I'm fed up!!! Now what?

Well, I'm sitting here drinking a 40 oz tripping off all this bullshit. I wrote a list of 10 things that I feel are stressing me out. I don't know what good it's going to do unless I go over each thing I wrote and evaluate it and make it work in my life in a positive way! Some of those things I don't even know how to make it positive. Off the subject though... I can't believe how much I like the SMELL of PUSSY!! I'm sitting here on my way to DRUNKVILLE, U.S.A. smelling Keisha's worn panties that she put in the dirty clothes hamper!! I remember when I was a kid about eight or nine and Jackie told me to smell her worn panties!! Ever since then I've had a fetish with the scent of pussy; worn panties.

Nowadays bitches be selling their worn panties on the internet!! SMH, lol!! I love smelling 'em, but I'm not about to buy a STRANGER'S worn panties just to please a fetish, lol. But frfr! I love the way pussy smells, taste, and feel! Fresh out the shower or the scent of the day! I love eating it until a woman cum so hard, she can't help but scream and squeeze my head between her trembling legs and I force them open until I'm done. I guess I'm a little horny. Hell, I haven't had any pussy since last Sunday! I've been back in California for a week and one day!! Yet, this BITCH Keisha claimed that she wanted me to come back because she missed me! Misery enjoys company!!!!

Journal insert

03JUNE1999: I'm sitting here in the parking lot of Smart and Final waiting to start work at 2:00 p.m. until 7:00 p.m. Only five hours and I'm glad because I really don't feel like working. Lord knows I need every cent of money I earn! Keisha is planning on moving on the 15th of this month. The other night we talked about how much we do not get along. Last night she asked if I mind having an open relationship, basically if we can see other people. I told her no and that when she moves, she can see whoever she wants. But while we are together that is not going to happen. **Maybe that would've actually worked if I was open-minded. Sounds like another polygamous "entanglement" opportunity that got thrown my way, but I was too naive to catch on back then. No would-haves, could-haves or should-haves. Everything happened exactly how it was supposed to — according to my Higher Power's will, the universe's directions, and the guidance of my ancestors.**

I told her also that I believe that she is already seeing someone else. She might not have fucked anyone else YET, but I believe she is seeing someone or interested in somebody. Same shit I've been through before. Can you believe this shit?!! Just like Destiny kept telling me before we separated that she wasn't fucking anybody, but I knew there was somebody and it was Boo Boo Yaw! Soon after I moved out of our house, she had that nigga in the house fucking him! I can't believe I'm going through this shit again!!! Except this time there ain't no love!!!

I went to court after I dropped Keisha off at work. I go in on the 6th of July for twenty days! I have to do this if I want to go to the Army. I feel like the Army is my only option. I've tried living by myself on "D" Street and I struggled. I tried living with mom, Blue, Barbara and Shirley, and even Destiny after we broke up!!! I tried marriage. True, I wasn't the man I was supposed to be. Maybe I can't because I was never taught how to be. I feel like I'm still a boy trying to be a man without a clue! I feel the Army is a chance for me to get my life in order and on a path in a specific direction. I hope to God this is something that I won't regret!!! Lord knows the few weeks ahead for me do not look too good!! My rent has not been paid yet. I still owe $200.00 because Keisha overflowed the tub twice. I owe Major $710.00 for putting my trip to New York on his credit card. I have to rent a truck and a storage room. After July 4th, I don't know where I'm going to live.

When I get out of jail on July 26th, I don't know where I'm going to live. I don't know how soon after I get out of jail the Army is going to send me down for my physical and then to boot camp!!!!! That's a whole lot on the stove. I don't even know if I have that many burners for all of that!!! I hope to God that I'm headed in the right direction. I'm not getting anywhere in San Bernardino County! I don't see Tomia that often. I'm not attending church service. My job is getting me nowhere. I don't advocate my money properly because it ain't that much or I live above my means too much. I cheated on Keisha five times and we ain't been married nine months yet!!!!!

She's cheated once, so she says, but she's ready to start seeing other people. She's slept in Tomia's room for the last couple of nights. She doesn't want to be with me or have sex with me. When we do have sex it's not all of that. I haven't fucked her since May 23rd, the day after I got back from New York!!! Even though I've been fuckin around I still be wanting to fuck her! But because she won't let me fuck, I fuck where I can and who I can. I know it's not right. Frankly, nothing's right at all right now!

Journal insert

15JUNE1999: Today I went to work from 5:00 a.m. until 12:00 p.m. Abdul dropped me off. Richard took me home. You're probably wondering why I didn't drive. Well, Sunday the 13th, Keisha moved out.

Journal insert

17JUNE1999: Yeah, Keisha moved out Sunday. **It was absolutely for the best. Our shit was really getting to the point where I wanted to put hands on her. One night, when Tomia was at our apartment, I was about to go hang out with Abdul to drink and smoke some bud. Keisha came running out of the apartment after me, holding Tomia's hand, yelling at me to take Tomia with me. That shit took me from 0 to 100 REAL QUICK! Mane, don't ever play with my children or drag them into our bullshit!**

She couldn't even be a "wife" and just chill with her "daughter-in-law" for a couple of hours! Instead, she literally ran out of the apartment, holding my daughter's hand and yelling. I ran up on her and asked, "What the fuck are you doing?" I didn't yell or holler, but I said it in a way she knew I wasn't playing games when it comes to my kids.

It took everything *—and I mean everything* **—inside of me not to choke the holy shit out of her right there in front of the apartment!**

And don't even get me started. One time, Auntie Pat told me that Rose and Violet weren't my real kids. I damn

near cursed her out! How the fuck could she say some shit like that when I was the one raising them? Meanwhile, her so-called friend abandoned them for fuckin drugs.

I digress...

With my consent, Keisha was allowed to take the car. She was supposed to have moved out on the 15th, but she came up to my job Saturday and took the car. I didn't know until she called me at work and told me. She said that she also found my journal in the car and was going to use it against me in court for the divorce. Well, it's not like I'm going to fight against the divorce. She said she was going to copy my journal, and I believe she said she was going to give a copy to the church. I talked to her on the phone. I told her to get her crap and get out of my apartment. I called Abdul and told him to go by my crib for me to make sure Keisha is not destroying my apartment. Abdul called me back at work and told me Keisha had a couple of guys at the apartment, and she couldn't get in because she lost her key. I thought about calling the manager and telling her not to let anyone in the apartment, but I didn't.

A couple of hours later, some thug came in Smart and Final. As soon as he walked in his eyes were on me. He walked closer to me. He told me that he wanted to talk to me outside. Looking like a menace to fuckin society! I told him that, "I don't know you, bro." He said, "But I know you." I told him to let me check with my manager. I went to the back and paged Abdul. He was only down the street when I paged him 911. He came in Smart and Final and told me the same guys that were at my apartment were outside the store with Keisha. Abdul told me that Keisha had on some cut off jean shorts looking like a hoochie. I was so pissed she had brought some niggas to my job. I was nervous and I definitely didn't want any bullshit at work. I left out the back of the store where Abdul met me. We went to his homeboy's house and picked up two of his homeboys. I went to Walmart and bought a lock for my apartment front door. Then we all went to my crib. I changed the locks on the door.

That night, I spent the night at Abdul's place. On Sunday, Abdul and I stopped by the police station so I could place a complaint. It wasn't anything the station could document. The officer told me I could write down what happened and keep it for my own personal records. Hell, I do that every time I write in my journal. We left there to go to my apartment. As soon as we were about to drive into the complex, Keisha was pulling out of the complex with a jeep packed with furniture following behind her car with the same nigga that came in my job. Abdul didn't pull inside the complex. He summoned them to follow us as we attempted to go by his homeboy house again. They didn't follow us, so we made a U-turn and followed them. We pulled on the side of the jeep. Abdul asked ol boy, "You wanted to talk to Thomas? Pull over so we can talk." Ol boy said, "I tried to talk to him yesterday at work." I told Abdul let's go check on my apartment because I was curious to know how the hell they got in.

When we arrived at the front door, we noticed that the doorknob was knocked completely off!!! I asked the neighbor to call the police for me. I went to the maintenance man's apartment. He had gone to a wedding in Rancho Cucamonga. Officer Walker arrived almost an hour after I called him. He told me and Abdul that it was not a burglary, and that legally I was wrong for changing the lock. She had been living in the apartment, and she hasn't given a thirty-day notice yet. I told the officer that I'm basically fucked! He agreed. He wasn't able to get the door open being that the top lock was locked, and I had left that key inside. Officer Walker told me to call back to the police station once I regain entrance if the apartment is destroyed or any of my belongings.

Journal insert

24JUNE1999: Well, I'm off work today. My clothes are drying in the dryer downstairs: four loads. There is still a lot of bullshit on my mind. Just dealing with the wrong people is taking a toll on me. Maybe I just run my mouth too fuckin much!! Yesterday Keisha called me asking why did I tell Barbara that she brought some dudes up to my job to fight me. **It was true, though. What I didn't tell Barbara was that Keisha had some niggas roll up on me at church while I was sitting on the church doorstep waiting for Bible study to start. Like, I bullshit me NOT! That bitch had some niggas run up on me at CHURCH! I was scared as fuck.**

How you come to a church to jump somebody? Niggas SMFH! Later on, I found out she was fucking one of 'em. Barbara is alright for an associate, but I really can't say she's a friend. Why would she continue to communicate with Keisha and tell her what I've told her!! To me, she would just listen to Keisha but not tell her what I've told her!! Keisha keeps telling me that the guy wanted to come to my job to get my permission to help her move. Whatever!! Like I told Keisha, if that was the case SHE could have come inside my job and asked me herself or called me and asked me! I am just too through!!! I'm done!!! I can't go on fucking with these same ol motherfuckas!!!! I'm tired of shit going around in circles! Keisha has my other journal. When she returns that, I will give her a check and I'm basically done with her. I'm done with Barbara because I can't trust her, and she isn't really there for me anyway. I'm through with Abdul because he's childish and full of shit and I don't like his wife.

Yesterday Abdul picked me up from work and we went by Judy (a female I met at work) and Brenda's, a friend of Shannon's, house. (*I thought you were through with Abdul but go on ....*) **Judy was a cute, short, petite, dark-skinned customer I met at Smart and Final. Brenda was also cute, short, petite, and dark-skinned. They were both lil hood rats —ghetto, but cool. They liked to drink, smoke weed, and FUCK. I enjoyed their company a lot because they were down-to-earth and real.**

We picked them up and went to my apartment. Abdul went into my daughter's room with Brenda to fuck her. When they came out of the bedroom, Abdul told me that he and Brenda were going to go pick up some weed at his place. But he didn't tell Brenda that it was at his place. So, he got to his apartment and knocked on the patio door, playing the role so Brenda wouldn't know he lived there. Come to find out his wife was home and my wife was there. He thought of a lie and told his wife to trust him, that there is a girl in the truck, and she just got raped up the street by Walmart. He told her that he had to take the girl to the police station. His wife tells him that she's going to the police station with them. He went to the truck first to tell Brenda to pretend that she just got raped. The shit is funnier by the minute. So,

Brenda offers Abdul's wife Lisa the front seat. Lisa took the back seat instead, looking at Abdul like she wanted to cut his throat. They got to the police station and Abdul walked Brenda inside.

Lisa offered to go but Brenda told them both that she'd be okay. Abdul told Brenda to call me and tell me what happened. She didn't have my number, so she called her house and had June to page Judy. I paged Abdul three times. He called my apartment. I asked him when he was coming over because Judy needed a ride back home. I asked him if it was going to be an hour. He said, "No." I asked, "Two hours?" He said, "No." I asked, "Three to five hours?" He said, "No." I asked, "So, what? You're not coming back?" He said, "No." I'm already pissed off now even more. June had already told Judy that my baby's mama was on her way to the apartment, my wife. I called my boy Kirk to help me out and come get Brenda. After Kirk left his mom's house, Abdul called from Brenda's house. He had the weed on him. Abdul said his wife was tripping at the apartment. So, he said he'll wait for me and Judy because Brenda had not made it there yet. When Kirk, Judy and I rolled up, Brenda was there. Kirk took off because he had to go to work. Abdul, Brenda, Judy and I went to the store to get something for Judy to roll the weed in and some chips.

We all went to the park and got high. It was funny because we were all sitting in the truck smoking and listening to music. Abdul got out of the truck and started dancing. He always makes me laugh when he dances. He got back in the truck, and kept asking us if we wanted to see him dance again. He kept saying that our wives were trying to set me and him up. Our wives kept telling him that he was paranoid, and he was tripping. Which he was slightly. After a while, we left to take the girls home. I tried to hug Judy, and she basically pushed me away! She said, "Not over here." What the fuck? Huh? She said she didn't have a man! So, what the fuck? When we were at my apartment, I tried to get some pussy from her before Kirk got there. You think she gave me some? Hell naw!!! I don't know what it is, but bitches be playing me for the fool!!!!

When I got home, I called this bitch name Fonda. You know how I play on the phone sometimes. So, I said, in my Barry White voice, "Hello, Fonda Green?" She said, "Who the fuck is this?" I said, "This is Barry White, and I want to know if you've been practicing what you preach?" Like the song, right? This bitch was like, "Who the fuck is this?" I told her, "It's me, girl. Thomas." She asked, "How do you know my last name?" I said, "Because you wrote it down when you gave me your number." What the FUCK!!! Do she think I fuckin looked it up in the phone book?!!! She told me that she didn't want me to call her anymore. I asked her, "What you got company or something?" She said, "I just don't want you calling me anymore." I said, "Fine." And we hung up the phone. I'm telling you, I'm sick of these California bitches!!!! It has got to be something in the fuckin water to make these tricks act the way they act. True enough Fonda and I got started on the wrong foot. She called Sunday and Violet answered the phone and said, "Who is this?" Fonda got a little aggravated. Then she called back later that night and Keisha ass answered the phone and wouldn't put it down after I picked up the other end.

I could barely hear Fonda so I just told her I would talk to her the next day. She told me she wasn't interested and hung up.

I called her back two days later and we had a good conversation. She told me already about her having a boyfriend and two kids. Two Asian dudes fathered her children. She's 22 and living in the projects on Waterman and Baseline. All I really wanted to do is just fuck the hoe anyway. I met her at work also. She was looking pretty good but fuck her as well. Judy said she was going to try to come through today. I haven't heard from her all day! I'm really discouraged but I'm trying to carry on. I know I shouldn't be fucking around anyway but I just don't know.

Journal insert

26JUNE1999: At this present time in life, I'm chillin at DeAdrian's, my homeboy and coworker from Smart and Final, house. He had to come pick me up from work because once again Keisha came up to my job tripping. She said she called the Internal Revenue Service (IRS), and they told her that they mailed her check out on the 8th of this month. Which is probably true. She wasn't going to get it until she returned this journal. It's apparent that this journal has been returned to me. She was straight trippin at Smart and Final. Just talking loudly and being ghetto!! Kim, one of my coworkers, told her she was going to call the police because we were in a place of business. The police told Kim that I should leave and not go home. I tried calling everybody to come and pick me up. I called DeAdrian and he was home chillin so he said he would come get me.

CHAPTER III

Sick of Being Lonely

· ◦ ● ◦ ·

Journal Insert
July 11, 1999

Well, I just woke up about 20 minutes ago. I fixed Tomia a bowl of cereal and cut us both a few wedges of cantaloupe also. She spent the night last night. Destiny picked me up from work which was cool. As you know, Keisha moved out on June 13th, I think it was. She tried to move back in once and, me as usual, didn't open my mouth and tell her no. That didn't matter because either the next day or the next two days she moved back out. Come to find out she was living with the rift-raft she had brought to my job. Then she moved home with me again and it didn't work out, so she moved with her mother. They got into it, and she moved back in with ol boy. He's been in jail since the 15th of June; only a few days after she moved in with him. Is that God working? Because I don't know. I talked to Jessie last night and he told me I should tell Keisha to come home. Jessie really don't understand that me and Keisha relationship is far from healthy!!! Maybe we will get back together, maybe not. It's God who has to rekindle us. I don't even think we were ever kindled! Let God's will be done not ours. I said that I'm not going to make any more major decisions without thinking it over!!!! I really have to mean that because I still find myself giving into things that I don't feel comfortable with!!!

I've been working a lot of hours lately. I will be able to pay Major off this week (thank God). He doesn't pressure me or anything. I'm just glad this debt will be over. I'm going to buy a used car next month, hopefully before my birthday. I'm just going to maintain 30+ hours a week and I'll be able to support myself and my daughter. I've decided that I should stop dealing with certain people also. Because like I told Destiny on the phone last night, I don't have any friends out here. Abdul is cool people but we are terrible for each other. A few weeks ago, Kirk, Abdul and I went and picked up this female I met at work along with two of her friends. We all kicked it at my apartment and went swimming. I screwed Judy, Abdul screwed Brenda, and Kirk didn't get to screw June. **June was cute, short, petite, and caramel complexion.** The next week, Abdul and I went to pick up Judy (the girl I screwed) and Brenda. Judy was acting shitty like she didn't want to go. We asked June, Judy's cousin. June wanted to go so we all went to my crib. We kicked it for a minute then June said she had to go home.

Living on my own. Now that Keisha moved out, I had my two-bedroom apartment to myself again. Our separation wasn't as near as heartbreaking as my breakup from Destiny. Mainly because

I did not love her as much if at all and I wasn't with her nearly as long. Abdul and I was hanging out even more. Smoking weed, drinking, dominos and card games, and fucking June, Brenda, and Toneka. My crib became the hang out spot. Somehow, I got in touch with Ms. J again, the transwoman that I met at the La Sex Shoppe in 1992. I hit her up one afternoon to see if I could swing by and see her; she gave me the okay. At this point, I had never been with a transwoman before. When I got to her house she was home alone. We sat in the kitchen choppin it up because we had not seen each other in a while. She was still fine as I remembered with that phat Rhythm Nation Janet Jackson ass! Shortly after catching up on things, we went to her bedroom.

As I was smashing her from behind, I reached to touch her penis, and she moved my hand away. As soon as she did that, I understood for some reason. I continued to smash until I got my nutt. She was kool people and I enjoyed chillin with her. The next time we chilled about a year later she looked different, like she was sick or something. As we chilled on the sofa at my place this time, I just could not help but feel that something was not right with her. I do not know if it was drugs or HIV/AIDS or if it was both honestly! I was turned off and was not going to take any chances even with a condom. I just did not feel right in my "Spirit" as they say lol, but frfr. She started rubbing my leg and asking me what was up. I just lied and told her that I was not feeling well and that I would take her back home. After that day, I never heard from her again.

Journal insert

13JULY1999: Yesterday I went to work from 11 a.m. until 7:30 p.m. I think I got home about 9:00 p.m. I made a few phone calls and called Mickey. I told him to come over. He brought me a beer and he was drinking on I believe rum and coke. As we sat down talking, we started kissing and he told me to take off my underwear and I did. I sat on top of him while he laid down. I lubricated his dick and then my ass hole. I put him in me and it was on!! He picked me up and he was taking me to a different level! It really felt good, and he came. He went and washed up and then I. He wanted me to come downstairs to see his new car. So, we went out and sat in his car talking for a little while. Mickey made a lot of sense. He was talking to me about his belief in God. Can you believe he told me to put God first and trust God as if I had a blindfold on and follow Him. Ask Him for the things I want. He was really deep, and if I'm not mistaken, I'm really starting to feel something special for Mickey. I'm so sick of the bullshit with women lately and he really feels like a breath of fresh air compared to Keisha, Destiny, Judy, Maxine, June, Renee, and that broad Fonda.

These females just frustrate me and even Abdul does. Sometimes I think Abdul wants to fuck me, but I don't want to go there. But I kinda do. I better not. Sometimes I find myself thinking about Abdul but today, I found Mickey heavily on mind!! Just the way we kiss, the way I rub his head and his face, feeling his beard, sucking his dick. He told me he loved me, and I told him I don't know what love is. I don't know what I'm doing but

I know I have to be careful! I have to keep working really hard because I have to get myself together.

Hours really have been good and this week I'll be able to pay Major off for sending me and Tomia to New York. I have to be wiser when it comes to money. It's all up to me. Keisha came up to my job today. She said she needed me to make her some copies, so I did because she said she didn't have any money. Then she asked me for five dollars. I told her I didn't have it, which I didn't. But if I had it, I would have given it to her regardless of Abdul telling me that Keisha told his wife that she was going to use me. If I had it, I would have given it to her because she had some things to do. So, Abdul took them back home.

Catherine had called me, and I was talking to her because she was in the process of moving back to Texas and needed me to help her load her truck the next day. Then the doorbell rang, guess who - Abdul, Brenda, and June. Abdul told me that Brenda was willing to have group sex. He wanted me to talk June into it. So, we came up with the plan that he would start making out with Brenda and then I would take over and then he would start making out with June. I got down on the living room floor with Brenda while June and Abdul were on the couch. I started sucking on Brenda's breast and unzipping her pants. Then Abdul interrupted us and told me that June said she was on her period. (I guess he figured since he couldn't fuck June, I couldn't fuck Brenda.)

I took June into the bedroom and started sucking her breast and pulled her pants and panties off. I started fucking and fucking her real good. I can't really remember if we smoked any bud that night, but I think we did. After a while Abdul came into the bedroom, and he took over. I went into the living room and started fucking Brenda bareback! But before I went in there, I remember while I was fucking Brenda in my living room, she was sucking Abdul's dick. Also, I remember Abdul smacking my ass while I was fucking June. It really was a crazy mixed-up night. I think I busted three nutts! Abdul saw me pounding the fuck out of June but I didn't get a look at him in action. I don't know if we will all hook up and do that again. I haven't fucked June since her, Brenda, and Abdul came over and spent the night Friday after we saw *Wild Wild West*. June didn't' want to fuck that night. I better be glad of that. She was saying her stomach was hurting. Her pussy was stankin!! I was horny as fuck too!! But I'm glad we didn't fuck. I saw her a couple times at the job, but she doesn't call or come up there to rap to me. Another case of female bullshit!! That night when her stomach was hurting, I told Abdul to let me fuck Brenda. He claimed that she said she didn't want to go there anymore. I think Abdul just didn't want me to fuck her! I know that I've been into some foul shit lately but I'm trying to do better. I guess I haven't ...

Journal insert

*21JULY1999 – 2:*29 AM: Wednesday: I'm just sitting here after smoking some weed with Mickey after letting him fuck me. He left about 40 minutes ago.

Journal insert

28JULY1999: I'm sitting here thinking about how unhappy I am with my life thus far. No, this isn't going to be another self-pity entry. Things just been unpleasing lately. I just came out of a pretty great weekend though. Saturday, I borrowed Rose's car and went to a Hawaiian themed party at Renee's house. It was pretty cool. Sunday, I went and picked up Tomia and then Kirk and his son Mike. We went to the Ontario Mils Mall. We all saw *Tarzan* at the movies. It was great. We then snuck in and saw *Star Wars*. It was good. Tomia was irritable and fell asleep. Monday morning, I went and picked up Violet. I was off and I still had Rose's car. I had a lot of chores to do around the apartment. I still had some movies from Blockbuster because I had company Sunday night; Brenda, June, and you know who. I did fuck that night, but I wasn't impressed. I would have rather masturbated. At least that way I'll be the only one involved in my nasty sins!!! I've got to get it together. I feel so sick right now physically and mentally. I talked to June today and she's not feeling well either. She said her stomach was upset and she threw up. I guess I would rather for her to be pregnant than to have a disease that either of us couldn't get rid of, especially AIDS!! I know there is going to be a punishment for my misbehaving!!

Journal insert

29SEPT1999: Well, it's been two months since I last wrote. I wrote about how unhappy I was with the way my life was going. Guess what? I'm still unhappy with the way my life is going. At this time, I am living around the corner from Smart and Final again. I call myself trying to save up for another car because I told Keisha to leave with the car we got together! I don't really give a flying fuck about that though. I just want my own fuckin ride!!! Once again, I'm tired of all these bitches in my fuckin life ... Keisha, Destiny, Renee, Maxine, and Jennifer. Even though Jennifer have not done me wrong yet, I just don't want to fuck with her. She's 50 and has eight kids. What the fuck could she be to me besides a fuck thing? And I don't even want that from her. **Jennifer and I ended up becoming really good friends over the years. It's been 23 years now. I fucked her about three times. I met Jennifer through her daughter, Angela. I was trying to fuck Angela, but she was on a whole different level that I was not fucking with—drugs. Rochelle then introduced me to Toneka, who was down to fuck, and that's how I met Angela's mother, Jennifer, in the process.**

I haven't heard from Mickey because I haven't called him. Yesterday Renee was supposed to come up to the job to pick up some boxes because her and her girlfriend are buying a house. (Now isn't that just special.) And no, I'm not playa hatin!! She didn't show up after work like we planned. Instead, she calls me at 7:15 p.m. after Smart and Final already closed. I made arrangements for us to meet up there and pick up the boxes. When I got dressed and got the apartment in order, because yes, I was anticipating on her

cumming over so I could fuck, (I'm lonely and I need companionship. That's all I can write), she fuckin pages me and tell me she has company at the house, and she can't make it.

She calls me today to pick them up and she came up to the job with her BITCH!!! Can you believe that shit!! She knew I wanted to fuck. Man, I'm sick and tired of being sick and tired of these BITCHES!!! All these HOES got somebody, but they keep fuckin with me, and I need somebody. (And not just anybody; I haven't gotten desperate!!) But all these HOES want to call me when they niggas, or in Renee's case bitch, is trippin. I'm tired of being here for they ass!!! I want somebody special in my life, male or female, just somebody that's real, honest, loving, understanding, caring, supportive, and respects me and appreciates me!!!!!!! I'm tired of being alone!!!!!!!

After all those years I am still faced with the same unwanted feeling of being alone.

Journal insert

30SEPT1999: Last night just as I finished my entry in my journal by writing, "I'm tired of being alone!!!!!!!", there was a knock at the door. Brenda and June! They came in and kicked it. We went to the corner store and got some cigarettes and another 40oz Old English beer. When we got back, I turned the music on, and June started dancing. I think it was turning Brenda on because she just kept acting silly and dancing behind June. Anyway, after a while, I had June strip down to her panties and then I danced with Brenda and stripped her down to her bare essence. I couldn't get hard enough to penetrate so I pulled the condom off (*niggas just don't learn*). Then as I grinded on Brenda for a few seconds, I started fucking her. I pulled June's panties off and started fuckin her. Brenda's pussy has always been better to me.

June asked for a cigarette while we were fucking so I let her get up and I started fucking Brenda again up until I nutted!! June got dressed and Brenda laid down and went to sleep. June left and went home, and Brenda spent the night. **Another opportunity for a polygamous relationship right in my hands and did not**

realize it. SMH! I know I have issues, and I really don't think that I'm going to live a long life. I try to get my life on track with God, but I don't try hard enough. I don't want to be a slave to sin, but I can't be lonely anymore. And I know I must be patient. I can't be happy. I know people say money cannot make a person happy if you are not already happy in your heart. But I think it sure can get me on the route to being happy. I think about my family's track record as far as marriage and it trips me out!!!

Journal insert

04OCT1999: Just to let you know, all days are not bad days. Yesterday was a pretty cool day. I really wish that I could have more days like that. I have to learn to take the bitter with the sweet. Yesterday started off with Rose lending me her car. First thing yesterday morning, I took her home, then I went and cleaned out all the trash in the car. I put all her personal stuff in a box and placed it inside of my apartment. I then found something to wear and took a shower. I got dressed and went to worship service at church. Only because Brother James Evans Sr. was preaching. He's a renowned preacher in the brotherhood of the church. I couldn't help but sit there hoping Keisha would show up. She never did.

After the service, I was running late because it was 1:30 p.m. and I was supposed to pick Tomia up at 1:00 p.m. Ya gotta love black churches lol. I drove to Smart and Final and purchased about four cases of apple cider that I promised Jessie I would buy for his wedding. I had to go to Destiny's mother's apartment to pick up Tomia. I didn't like the shorts Tomia was wearing because they were too short. I also didn't like the shirt she had on because it was too loose. Other than that, she was ashy. Destiny said it was Tomia's fault that she was ashy because she was playing on the carpet with her half-sister and not yet brother-in-law.

Tomia was reluctant to leave because she was enjoying her time there. I told her to just stay. Then I went to pick up Jesse's homeboy Mac in Fontana. Mac's in the wedding also. Mac and I went to Los Angeles to attend the rehearsal dinner. I thought we were extremely late because we were supposed to be there at 3:00 p.m. We got on the freeway about 2:45 p.m., arriving there in good time about 4:00 p.m. When we arrived, they blessed the food, and everybody ate. The food was off the HOOK!! Sandra's, Jesse fiancé, dad barbecued the night before.

Journal insert

07OCT1999: I'm sitting here waiting to get started with the rehearsal for Jesse and Sandra's wedding. I'm in Los Angeles at the church they are planning to get married in. It really is a beautiful church. I think it's an excellent place to get married considering getting married where I did. Which is where Keisha and I got married!!! Because she couldn't wait, and I wasn't man enough to make her wait or tell her to get on about her business. Now we're separated. One year and about a week later our marriage went to shit! Another statistic I'm branded with.

Journal insert

09OCT1999: I just finished masturbating about 15 minutes ago. As usual I feel depressed!! I wrote before that my life is a mess, and

I still feel that way. I'm not a happy camper!! I'm a slave to sin. People outside the church would probably say that there is nothing wrong with masturbation. Some even say there's nothing wrong with homosexuality, especially Ricki Lake fat ass. I'm not happy with it or comfortable with it or want it in my life: masturbation, homosexuality, or bisexuality! Jesse told me yesterday after I asked him if masturbation is a sin that it is! I still did it! True enough we sin every day. Sometimes knowing and sometimes unknowingly! I think and believe that I'm a sex addict!! I'm so sick of drinking, smoking, and sinning!!

I don't even think I have enough will or discipline to stop! I've thrown away packs of cigarettes and poured out beer in attempts to quit but I always go back to it! I don't want to die like this! I keep thinking about that song *Family Affair*, the part when it says the other brother was made to burn. I don't exactly know what the writer meant. But I feel that the writer meant that one was made to maybe go through trails or made to burn in hell. I don't think anyone could tell me that someone is placed on earth to be destined to go to hell. From my understanding Judas, an apostle of Jesus, was made to betray Jesus. I understand that he was handpicked to go to hell.

I believe in the Old Testament. It was prophesied that Jesus or the Messiah would be betrayed. I don't know but this is just my understanding. I'm tired now and it's 3:03 a.m. I guess I'll try to sleep now. Before I do, I'm going to rid myself of the rest of the cigarettes I have. I hope to God I never smoke another one. I'm also going to pour out the rest of the beer and hope to God that I never feel that I need or want another buzz. I hope and pray

I never masturbate again or fornicate again. Only God knows how I truly feel right now. Throwing away cigarettes, pouring out alcohol, and the guilt that followed masturbating became a vicious cycle of self-torture. My sexual identity turmoil added to my own self suffering. I prayed, hoped, and wished it all away over and over; constantly and frequently all to no avail. Years became two decades of a war inside of me that no one was aware of.

Journal insert

11OCT1999: I just got in from Los Angeles about an hour ago. I went out there early Saturday morning about 1:30 a.m. I was one of the seven groomsmen that Jesse had in his wedding Saturday. It was a beautiful wedding! The other groomsmen and I rented a limousine. It was really nice. I thank God for the experience, and I hope to God Jesse and Sandra have a beautiful, loving, respectful, long lasting harmonious marriage! **Twenty-three years later, and they are still wonderfully married. It's strange how, when I wish the greatest for other people's relationships, they seem to thrive. Meanwhile, I've been wishing, hoping, and praying for the same for myself, but all I've found is heartache, disappointments, and depression.** I count Jesse as a good friend of mine. We've only known each other for a few years but I've learned and am learning to respect him. I believe he has helped me a great deal with his spiritual advice. I know he isn't perfect because none of us is perfect, but he displays the way a young Christian man should carry himself.

Sandra is a really sweet young lady. Jesse and Sandra look beautiful together. Sometimes I think about Jesse's life, and I wonder why God has allowed MY life to be so different. Jesse's dad has always been a major part of his life and so has his mother. He completed college. His family bought him a car. Jesse played sports in school, and I think even in college. Women find him attractive and flock to him. Before he became a Christian, he had more than his share of women. He became good friends with Sandra and after a few years he married her without ever having sex with her, from my understanding. Today they are flying to Hawaii for their honeymoon, and that was a gift to them. Believe me when I say, there is no jealousy, envy or anything of that nature in my heart. I am truly happy for the both of them. Thing is ... I want to be happy too!!

Journal insert

13OCT1999: I'm home basically trying to occupy my time while my spirit and flesh fight it out. I really want a cigarette and a beer. I could go for some sex as well but I'm not going to press my luck. If I am to do this right, I won't be having sex for a long time. Keisha paged me from her job today, but I didn't call her back. I'm really trying to move on with my life without her. It's like Jesse told me the other day, "Keisha does not add joy to my life only stress. She does not show any signs of having the fruits of the spirit!" I know I don't show many signs of the spirit, but I try. At this time, Keisha feels that the grass is greener on the other side. At least that's what I think she feels. She's on her own. I have to get me in order!!! It's so hard and I know it's not going to happen overnight, or is it? I have to start some time!! It's just really hard being by myself. No real friends around, no car, not even a good female friend to just talk to. I am so alone! Isolated. I know that I should try to enjoy my solitude because I may not always have it but it's just so hard for me right now.

Journal insert

14OCT1999: I'm sitting outside of my apartment on a chair that used to belong to a dining room set that Renee gave me five years ago. Thinking about how weak I am. I'm drinking a beer and smoking a cigarette. I know I wrote that I have to stop but I know I can't do it overnight. Damn it, I have to stop!! Today was pretty cool. Destiny brought Tomia over this morning before she went to work. Being that the cable is off, Tomia watched a video tape of hers until she fell asleep. We both got up about 11:00 a.m. Jennifer called me as I was waking up. I talked to her briefly. I really wish she would get the hint and stop calling me. I know I messed up when I had sex with her. If I haven't told you, she is literally old enough to be my mother! I'm just not interested. Mickey's been paging me; not today or yesterday, but recently and it's driving me crazy! I'm so hungry for companionship and horny but I want to better my life as a Christian! I want to remain celibate until me and Keisha get our acts together or until I remarry. I really don't think I can do it!

I took Tomia to the mall. We took pictures together. I like the way they came out. Tomorrow I'm going to send mom some of the pictures. After Tomia and I took pictures, we went to the movies and saw *Inspector Gadget*. Tomia liked it, I didn't. As long as she enjoyed it, that's all that mattered to me. Then we had an ice cream sundae at Baskin Robbin's, just like Destiny and I used to get banana splits from Baskin Robbin's. I took her to my job after Baskin Robbin's to show my coworkers the pictures. When we were done at the job, we walked to my apartment, then we caught the bus to Blockbuster. I rented a couple of videos. I used my credit card to purchase *The Prince of Egypt* for Tomia. Once we returned to my apartment, I called moms in New York. I let Tomia talk to her. When Tomia was done talking to moms, I reluctantly went and charged a beer, a pack of cigarettes, and a couple of bags of chips to my credit card. I want to go and get a dildo so bad! Last night when I was feeling this way, I picked up my bible and I felt much better. But I just don't think that's going to be the remedy every time I feel this way. I guess I won't know until I try to pick it up and read it every time I feel this way. It's so hard. So lonely. I don't won't to die this way! I need a car so badly, but I don't even think that would help me out now. Only God can help me help myself. I am weak!

CHAPTER IV

I Was Born This Way

· • ◉ • ·

Journal insert

04OCT1999 – 12:57 AM: I just finished smoking a cigarette once again. I really didn't want to buy another pack, but I guess I did because I did. I spent another lonely evening watching home videos and drinking a beer. Jesse called and I was glad to hear from him. He enjoyed his honeymoon in Hawaii. He said that it's really overrated. We talked for a little while. I'm really happy for him. Abdul came by the job yesterday. I really love him. I don't know why but I do. He's so funny to me. As I was working on the register helping customers, he kept talking about how much he misses me. He kept saying that he loves me in front of the customers. I know they probably thought we were gay or something. Abdul is just a trip. He knows I'm in turmoil with my sexuality, but he says stuff like that to me. The things he used to do in front of me make me wonder about his sexual preference. Renee paged me yesterday. I didn't return her page, and she called me. She basically wants me to help her move. I told her as a friend I'll help her. I'm not trying to get in her panties anymore. I'm tired of the frustration.

Journal insert

*20OCT1999 – 8:*49 PM: I feel and felt pretty good today. This week I'm aiming for 40 hours. That will cover rent next week and allow me to get Tomia's layaway out for school. I talked to Destiny this morning after having another dream about her last night. She was telling me about the car auction. She got her car from there for about $900 and her mom got a car from there for about $250. I think that it will be best for me if I go there to purchase a car. I really don't want or need a car note right now. I've finally reached a point, thank God, that I can afford my rent with one check and still have change! I plan to start paying off my bills next month and buy a car! I'm tired of my self-pity! I'm ready to live and take charge of my life!! I hope and pray to God that I haven't damaged my body by the sexual choices I've made.

I don't want any more sexual transmitted diseases or get AIDS, and I don't want cancer. I want to live a long healthy Christian life. I'm excited because I know a change is coming for ME! I'm going to blow up into a whole new life. Like a caterpillar changes into a butterfly. I'll be 30 next year and I'm hoping that it's going to be better than my teens and twenties. I'm hoping it will be the start of my manhood, independence, and my spiritual confidence! **Let's break it down: my teen years, ages 13 to 19. From 14 to 15, Crystal Rae was my girlfriend. From 15 to 16, I was with Evelyn. From 16 to 17, Kenya was my girlfriend. Then, from 17 to 22, I was with Destiny.**

This brings me into my early twenties through 29. From 22 to 28, I was single for six years. I got married to Keisha at 28, and we stayed married until I was 32, when our divorce was finalized.

Journal insert

29OCT1999: I'm sitting here not too happy with my life once again. I just finished masturbating with a dildo again. Instant gratification, no love involved. Just like fornicating! I'll give you the reasons why I should be happy and the reasons why I'm not happy. First,

I'm living, I'm able, I'm working, I have my own apartment (that I can well afford working part-time), I have a decent job, I'm attractive (at least I think so and a few other people think so), I'm young (Rod Stewart's song *Forever Young* just reminded me of that), my children are living, they're healthy, my mom and brother are living (I hope they're healthy). Well, those are a lot of things and reasons to be happy about but I'm not. I'm not happy because I don't have a car to be able to see my daughters whenever I want. To be able to take them to different places, do things with them, and spend time with them.

I'm not happy because I'm not living happily ever after with my wife! I'm not happy because I feel that I'm abusing myself, my temple, by constantly masturbating and with an artificial DICK! I don't know what really happened in my childhood besides, of course Wolf, but I can't be gay not even bisexual. I remember Wolf fucking me when I was at least nine years old, but I don't remember any sexual encounters before then with the same sex.

It seems so cliché to say, "I was Born This Way." What else could I say or believe? Who do I blame?!!!!?? I don't know what "life" is about! But I know I call myself a Christian and I believe God is against homosexuality and fornication. At least that's what the bible tells me.

I realize that the bible may have been changed over time, of course, but I just can't believe that homosexuality is okay or bisexuality. I was telling my friend Pascal, a coworker from Smart and Final, at work today that I want to live where I am until I finish college, then I want to move to the mountains and buy me a Toyota 4-Runner. Become a teacher or have some sort of career and live there without television. I do have future plans, but the bible tells me not to get adjusted to this world. But this world is all I know, and I know our stay here is brief. But I have to plan some sort of future. I do want more children. I do want a wife. I do want a new home and a new car, but I just don't see it. I just don't feel it. To show God that I do want these things, I will throw away my cigarettes, my beer, my dildo, and stop masturbating. I don't know what I'm going to do to get by except read the bible. That's my only source that can get me through. May my God I have faith in get me through.

For 23 years, I grappled with alcohol, cigarettes, marijuana, my sexual identity, masturbation, and even masturbation with an artificial penis. The desires to do those things were powerful and overwhelming mentally, eventually becoming physically disastrous when alcohol use spiraled into abuse and damn neared ended me. I had no one to truly talk to —partly because I was embarrassed, and partly because I was ashamed. I didn't feel that I could trust anyone with such intimate, sensitive details about my life.

I was a "MAN" damn it! I was strong! A strong BLACK MAN! I wasn't a "punk" or a "faggot"! See, in my community, especially among "MY" people —black people — a bisexual black man isn't seen as just that. Bisexual black women, on the other hand, are often viewed as sexy, erotic, and accepted —unless the woman is a hard-core stud. Even then, studs are only slightly frowned upon compared to the outright disdain for black gay or bisexual men. Many of my people view a black bisexual man as simply gay —a punk, a faggot, a nigga with sugar in his shoes.

I remember being a teenager, talking on the phone with this grown-ass lady who told me I sounded like I had sugar in my shoes —LMAO! I knew exactly what she was implying, and it hurt my feelings deeply. Now, as an adult, I know better than to concern myself with what people think about me. But as an impressionable child, adolescent, and young adult, without anyone to love me or teach me self-love, self-expression, and self-worth, I sought it out elsewhere.

I sought to be loved, valued, and appreciated through four vital relationships and countless sexual encounters with both women and men.

Journal insert

01NOV1999: I've been off work for about an hour. Now I'm sitting here listening to

Whitney Houston (Brown). I just cracked open a can of beer. Since I've been home, I've been thinking about calling Mickey. He's been paging me a lot lately, but I won't return his calls. Every time he calls me, well page me, it's always late at night. I know all he wants to do is fuck me. I probably should have a relationship with Mickey. Just to try something different. But that would be too much! What would my daughters think?! What if they think it's okay to be gay? Like Ricki Lake ass think! I talked to Jesse, one of my closet friends that I met at church back in 1996. I was also one of his groomsmen in his wedding October of this year, last night. I talked to moms yesterday as well, only about my frustrations not about Mickey of course!! Moms just tells me to be patient and Jesse told me the same thing basically.

Sometimes I love talking to Jesse because he helps me so much. But I can't help the way I feel. It's just hard sometimes to shake this feeling of wanting to be with a man or a woman. I want to be with a woman more, but I can't, I can't!! My spirit and my flesh, between the two, where am I?? I don't know if I'm just lacking being patient, I guess I am. Even though the bible tells Christians not to look at what the people of this world has. I just find it hard to just be satisfied. I'm human and I want things too!! I paged Keisha yesterday and she called me back at the job. I told her that my refrigerator had been out for a few days and that I was at work hungry. She told me at first that I had the nerve then she told me she was at Stater Brother's buying her some BBQ chicken and that I could have some of hers. I told her that was fine. She rolled up to my job. New rims on the car and a new stereo. She had her hair done and yeah that did bother me.

Yeah, I know I told her to leave, and it still bothered me. Like I told my mom yesterday, that it just doesn't seem or feel right. It seems like I'm always getting the shorter end of the stick!! Everybody wants me to be patient, but I tell you until I do get my bank account fat and my new car and the clothes and style I want, I just think my attitude towards certain individuals is going to be BITTER!!! But to a lot of individuals, I owe them a lot of love because they were truly there for this here negro! I really wanted to see where my wife's head was, and I still think "She's a BITCH", as Missy Elliot said. My wife doesn't realize I'm "Bad By Myself", as said by TLC!! Watch me blow the FUCK UP!!

Journal insert

05NOV1999: Today would've made 11 years for me and Destiny if we didn't break up. Oh well. I'm sitting here listening to Elton John's *Love Songs* CD. Tomia's sleeping. I worked 40 hours this week. This makes three weeks in a row! I told you the hours were good. I bought another refrigerator today. I hope and pray that it lasts a long time. This morning, I woke up about 7:00 a.m. with a slight hangover. Last night, Kirk and I went to this club called The Elks Lodge. We had fun. This older lady named Tanya wanted me to meet her there last night. She kind of reminds me of my mother. We didn't hook up or anything. As a matter of fact, I didn't even see her for the rest of the night I was there.

It really was a cool lil outing. I let Davis and his girlfriend Latoya spend the night. I met Davis while working at Smart and Final, he was the security guard there. They're having problems finding a place to live. They had been sleeping in Davis's pickup truck. He has a camper shell over the bed of his truck. It was a pretty disturbing night beside the point that I was a little intoxicated. Davis's slight snoring and his girlfriend's, who is very overweight and about 20 years younger than Davis, loud snoring disturbed me deeply. I don't know if all obese people snore like that or what. But I know Blue used to snore like that too and he's also very heavy. Anyway, I got up, took a shower, then went to the job to pick up my check. I went to 7/11 and bought a much-needed V8. Afterwards, I caught the bus downtown San Bernardino and deposited some of my check because I had to keep some cash for the refrigerator.

Then I treated myself to breakfast at Molly's Cafe. When I first walked in, I started to walk right back out. I thought it was a hick hang out until I saw a couple of Negros in there **lol**. I was seated and I ordered. I really needed that breakfast. I felt good being by myself there because some of my sistas and brothas probably couldn't dig a place like that. **It was like a smaller version of Cracker Barrel**. When I was done eating, I went and bought the refrigerator. Then I went home to get some things out of the way for the refrigerator. I went to work for eight hours, and we were BUSY!! Destiny picked me up from work. Me, her, and Tomia went to Marshall's so I could put some money on Tomia's layaway.

I also bought me some much-needed pants. While I was at work, I bought some groceries to fill my new refrigerator. This is the third refrigerator I bought from Lucky Buy. Elektra (Ellie) just called. I don't know if I've mentioned her in the past. She's an old friend. I don't remember how we met or where. She has a caramel complexion, nice body, nice natural long hair, kind of like

Destiny's hair. When I met her, she was living in the Waterman Garden's projects on Baseline and Waterman with her, I believe, three children. We've never had coitus and right now I'm not going there. I'm trying to do better in the choices I make.

Journal insert

11NOV1999: I'm at the bus stop waiting for the bus. I just left the gym from working out. I figured that I really need to start occupying my days off and extra time with something positive. I came down to the gym and got a membership for $197. I know that sounds like a lot of money that I don't have. I really think I need to start working out again. I know that it's a commitment and I'm not too good with commitments. I think it's about time for me to start feeling better and looking better! I'm going to work extra hard to make up the money I spent. Even though I was able to give them, 24 Hour Fitness, a check today for $100 and a postdated check for $97.00 I still want a car but not just any car. I'm going to try to save about $2000 and then get one.

I'm going to at least try to go to the gym three times a week or more. I'm trying to relax and enjoy my life by taking it easy; one step at a time. After I finished working out, I bought a protein bar that Sal, the employee at 24 Hour Fitness that sold me the membership, recommended. Man, that protein bar tasted like chocolate covered DIRT MUD!!! It was thick, chewy, and heavy!! I'll have to try a different bar next time and it was $3.50!! I feel good after the work out. I always do and sometimes horny but not this time. I've been feeling a little better about myself and life lately. I still drink and smoke. I do want to stop smoking and just have a drink every now and then but it's hard. That's another reason why I joined the gym. I don't know if I wrote that me and Kirk went to this club called The Elks Lodge last Thursday or not. But we did and we had fun.

We will probably go again tonight. When I get home, I'm going to call Lameka. I don't remember if I wrote anything about her or not. I met her at work. I took down her number off her check and called her last Saturday. I went up to her job Monday and tonight I'm going to call her and ask her out. I talked to Sister Pat, from church, last night and she told me that women basically like to be pursued. The thing about me is if they don't show me that they're interested, I don't pursue! Sister Pat told me that women don't usually call men because they don't want to seem desperate. I'll take her word for it and call Lameka. Renee came by last night to pick up her work badge she left a couple of weeks ago. We had a long, good talk and I hope it did both of us some good. We've been friends for a long time, and I hope that we can remain good friends.

Journal insert

13NOV1999: Once again, I'm at the bus stop. This time I'm on my way to the gym. I really need to go because I'm so upset I just want to snap. I know I don't really have any true reason to be so angry. I'm just frustrated with a lot of things besides missing the bus and having to wait 30 minutes for another one. I decided to use this time to write about my frustrations. I'm tired of being stuck on STUPID!! I just want a car. That's what it boils down to. I'm tired of planning on going out and my ride FLAKES!!

I'm tired of catching the bus. Guess what? The bus just came. I'll write more later.

Now I'm downtown San Bernardino waiting on my second bus. I feel a little better. I just need to get out of the apartment for a little while. If I can't be happy with myself and enjoy my life, how could I add to someone else's happiness?? I'm trying to find ways to occupy my time and enjoy the time on earth that I have been blessed to have. The complaints have to stop. Like Outkast said, "You got to get up get out and get something."

I'm going to continue to try no matter. I got to. So what if Lucas sees Tomia more than I do? So what if I don't have a car right now to pick her up as often as I'd like? That's EXACTLY my POINT, "as often as I like." Sometimes Tomia wants to stay home. Sometimes she doesn't even want to come with me. She has a little sister at home by Destiny and Lucas. And sometimes Lucas's son comes over there and spends time there. This weekend Destiny's getting a house, renting one. So now Tomia will have a nice big yard to play in and plenty of space to run around and be with her family. Yeah, I know that I'm her family too, but they say home is where the heart is. She has everything to keep her happily busy at home. I am soooo sore from working out at the gym on Thursday. The only thing that I'm going to do is try to enjoy my life. I love Tomia and I'll do whatever God allows me to do. I can't get blood from a turnip, as granny always used to say. I hope my time is coming. The time when I'm satisfied, content, happy, and just enjoying life. I know there will always be things that bother me but those things I'm not going to dwell on too long. Like I wrote before, "I can't get blood from a turnip."

Journal insert

*19NOV1999 – 3:*08 AM: I just got in a little while ago from The Elks Lodge. I drove Rose's car and took Kirk with me. It was cool. Nothing really to write about. I saw some cute women and some cute guys. After I drove home, and Kirk took off in his car, I went to the adult store down the street. I bought a dildo and a video tape. Yeah, I know, here I go again. And before I went to the club, I bought a pack of cigarettes. I wasn't planning on it. I was going to go down the street to the doughnut shop and buy a couple of single cigarettes, but I had Kirk waiting long enough so I just went to 7/11 and bought a pack.

I just finished masturbating and as usual I don't feel too thrilled!! Before I bought the dildo, I said in my mind, *I'm not going to throw it away.* I used the money Renee loaned me yesterday to buy an outfit for the Soul Train Awards Tuesday. My children make me angry because of their irresponsibility and I use the money a friend loans me to purchase something for my instant gratification! Cheap thrills, no FEELS! True enough it felt good but now I feel still incomplete.

Sunday night, I saw Keisha at church. We talked when she came and sat next to me on the back pew in the church. I saw Abdul and his wife. I wanted to be mean and call his wife something, but I can't. Anyway, after I got home Keisha called me and wanted me to come over to her apartment, so I did. If I didn't tell you, she got an apartment about a month ago. I kicked it with her. She wasn't feeling well, and she was on her period. I wasn't planning on having sex with her anyway. I did bring condoms just in case and also my bible. We talked for a while, and she wanted me to stay the night because she CLAIMED to be scared. Just as I figured - her rift-raft had been staying with her and of course they weren't getting along. She told me she had to call the police on him.

See I knew it couldn't just be me. Keisha can't get along with anyone. Her mom, me, or her rift-raft boyfriend. She tells me still, "You haven't changed." She said that because when she picked up some papers from my apartment for her speech at school, she saw a picture of Destiny and I on my entertainment center along with over ten other pictures. I don't know what Keisha wants from me. She did tell me she wants to be spoiled. She doesn't want her man to ask her anything about her money, she wants a home with a washer and dryer so she doesn't have to haul clothes, and she only wants to take care of small bills. I guess that's fine and dandy being that I am supposed to be the man and I am suppose take care of my wife. She was even asking me personal things about my sex life. I guess she felt that I was supposed to tell her because she told me about what she's been doing. People trip me out with shit like that.

They want you to do because they do! True enough we are to treat people how we want to be treated but we are not obligated to treat people how they treat us! Now I think that's deep. I don't tell people things so that they can tell me things and I don't do for people so that they can do for me. God knows the motives of our hearts. That's deep too. It's 3:41 a.m. and I know I should be asleep because I have to attend a store meeting at 5:30 a.m. I know that it just might be very interesting, especially if anyone at work heard me on the radio last night on 99.1 FM. When I got up to start getting ready to go out to the club, I turned the radio on.

The DJ announced that if anyone was pissed off about something to call in. I picked up my phone, but I couldn't remember the number to 99.1. Then the DJ gave out the radio number. I called and the line wasn't busy!! The DJ answered and he asked me what was I pissed off about. I told him, "I'm pissed off because my manager only hires his

friends and people he knows. He doesn't hire African Americans or people in the community." The DJ put me on the air. I only had ten seconds to talk. I got on the air and said, "I'm pissed off because my boss only hires his friends and people he knows, and he doesn't hire African Americans or people in the community." I thought that was all the DJ was going to air, but he also aired the question he asked me. He asked me where did I work and I told him Smart and Final. Before I told him why I was pissed off, I told him my name and that I was from San Bernardino. Anyway, if anybody from work heard it, they know it was me. Whatever happens, happens. God's will, will be done.

Journal insert

19NOV1999: I just got in from the store meeting. I couldn't put Major, my boss, on front street in front of everybody. I talked to him in his office. I told him that I don't think that the store is a place of equal opportunity and that he hires whom he knows and pleases. He was offended and maybe a little hurt. I could tell. He told me that he is not racist. **Ain't that the first thing that a racist say? Ijs, SMH!** I told him I didn't believe he was racist.

Major went on to tell me that my work habits this week were very poor. **Prime example of DEFLECTING, but I did not realize that then.** I noticed on next week's schedule before he told me about my work habits, I only had two days of work; 10 HOURS!! He stated that it was because of my poor work performance this week. After our talk, I asked him if I could have more hours being that I have rent coming up the following week.

At first, he had the attitude like that's a "YOU" problem but he said he would give me a couple of more days. Then he told me that I bring my problems to work, and I don't pick up speed and that I'm pretty much laxed. I told him that I recently joined the gym and I've probably been a little tired because of fitting that in my schedule. I'm going to tell myself that I'm not smoking anymore!! Once again, I've thrown away a new pack of cigarettes. I'm going to go to work leaving my problems at home. I'm not going to complain about anything to anyone. I'm going to try my best to stay busy as long as I'm there! No attitudes with customers. If they have a problem, I will direct them to management! I just want to get my ass back in school so that I can get a real fuckin job! Something I can be proud of and enjoy doing. I'm a slave for Smart and Final.

Major was going on about how great a company Smart and Final is. That's TO HIM and FOR HIM!! He makes $1000 a week plus bonuses and other perks probably!! He also told me he hasn't seen me give my full performance and that I'm up and down and not consistent. That may be true because this is not a career move for me, just a stone to step on to reach my goal!!! I've dedicated six years of my life to Smart and Final so far. I am appreciative.

I'm very grateful because I was working at McDonald's when I landed the job at Smart and Final. I've given them blood, sweat, and literally tears throughout the years. When I was at the store in Santa Monica, we got robbed three times at gun point.

I remember the first time the store got robbed scared the shit out of me. A guy ran into the store and attempted to jump over the chain that was up to block entry between the registers. The attempt was in vain because he fell over the chain. I was the closing cashier. I looked down at him and asked him if he was okay. He jumped up and pointed a gun in my face. I immediately put my hands in the air. He yelled at me to put my hands down, I believe because he didn't want anybody outside to see what was going on inside the store. I put my hands down and gave him the money out of my till. While this was going on with me, another robber was in the office with the manager on duty getting money out of the safe. True indeed a very terrifying event for me. I was so shaken up and scared I had to call Aunt Lois to pick me up. I never got counseling, therapy, or any help with that which lead to Post Traumatic Stress Disorder.

CHAPTER V

Do Me Baby

· ◦ ◉ • ·

Journal insert

*25NOV1999 – 2:*19 PM: Maxine just left about 20 minutes ago. She came (more than one way) over last night about 12:00 a.m. When I got in from work, well actually after I came in after church, I paged her, and she called me back. We made arrangements for her to cum over. She wanted to make some White Russians (mixed drinks), so I went to the liquor store and bought some gin, Kahlua, milk, and a pack of cigarettes. She came over about 12 a.m. and we talked for a while. Then she went and took a shower. We talked about a lot of things, about her experiences as a child and why she's bisexual. I told her about my experiences and told her that I was bisexual as well. I've been knowing that she was bisexual since last year, but I never told her about me until last night. I only told her because she has been a pretty good friend of mine for about four years and a couple of months, and I felt comfortable with her. It's really a trip to me that she is way more understanding than Keisha.

Renee is also very understanding. I know it's because Maxine and I have experienced same sex encounters in our early years and because Renee and I have had experiences with same sex as adults. I was watching the movie *Living Out Loud* the other day and Queen Latifah said something that really caught my attention. She said in the movie that, "She always knew her boyfriend was gay and that he is really understanding and lovable but he just likes sucking dick." That might not be exactly what she said word for word but that sums it up.

Anyway, when Maxine got out of the shower, she had on her little G -string outfit that glowed according to the black lights I had on. She started dancing for me (thick, rich, and chocolate .... mmm good). As I lay on the bed, she got on top of me, smelling like the route to ecstasy. She sucked my dick better than I can remember it ever being sucked. We fucked hard and long. I guess it was the gin that made me sin (Ya know I'm not serious about that) I came good!!! And fucked her for at least another 30 minutes until she came. We went to sleep about 5:00 a.m. Maxine woke up a few hours later to use the bathroom. When she got back in the bed, we fucked again, hard and long. She came first. Then I changed positions a couple times and fucked her hard while sweating bullets baby!!! It was hard pleasurable work, but I shot my load on her ass and back!!!

Afterwards we took a shower together. As the warm water rained on our naked bodies Maxine dropped to her knees right down before me in the shower and began sucking my dick. She sucked my balls and licked my ass hole while sticking her tongue in and out of it. **That was the first time I'd EVER had my**

**"salad tossed" or my "groceries ate," as they call it, lol —
and it definitely wasn't the last time.** She was really taking
me there. She kept telling me she wanted me to cum over her face
and titties. I told her, "I can't cum from oral sex." She responded
with, "We have to work on that." OKAY!! We talked about our
lives after we got out of the shower. We talked about some deep
issues: our grandmother's passing was really deep. She feels that
her grandmother's death should had been prevented because her
aunts should have taken her to the hospital after having a slight
stroke. Maxine's gone now.

She's going to Oceanside to spend time with her family for
Thanks-For-Giving-Us your land day. I've paged Rose several
times today so that I could use her car so I could do some visits
also. Her ass ain't called back yet!! She called me earlier while
Maxine and I was fuckin, and I told her to call me in an hour. So,
I told her also that I wanted to go somewhere, and she basically
was complaining about her wanting to go to different places
also. And she told me happy Thanksgiving when I answered the
phone. Yeah, whatever, my time is coming. She just pissed me off
due to her fuckin complaining and unwillingness to help me out
because I don't have a car.

I wasn't fuckin asking to keep the fuckin car all day, I just
wanted to visit a few people while she visited a few people. But
fuck it, fuck her car, fuck her, and fuck the pony she rode in on.
My day is dawning. That's all I can say or write, my day is dawning!
I was invited to four different events. Barbara's house, DeAdrian's
house, Destiny invited me to come to Aunt Pat's house, and
Barbara invited me to come to Rosa house with her for a minute.

Ya think Kirk invited me to kick it with him knowing I don't have my family out here or have a car? Yeah, my day is dawning. I'm going to smoke another cigarette and take a nap. Once again, I wish to all a Happy Thanks-For-Giving-Us your land day!

Journal insert

*25NOV1999 – 6:*17PM: I am sooo pissed off I don't know what to do except drink this White Russian drink I've made and it's mmmm mmmm GOOD! I just got in from walking my ass to Stater Brother's to write a check for cashback as Elektra recommended. The mother fuckers wouldn't approve me for cash, so I just wrote a check for some orange juice and walked my black lonesome ass back home. Barbara just called. She'll be over in about 15 minutes. Therefore, I'm going to smoke a cigarette and drink my drink before she gets here. I'll write later.

Journal insert

25NOV1999: I just got in from Barbara's apartment. She came and picked me up. She rented the movie *Skeletons*. We watched it. It was cool. What was coolest is that she fixed me a fat plate of Thanksgiving dinner and I grubbed! Especially being that all I had eaten all day was a honey bun and a glass of milk. The evening turned out good. I know I was pretty hot earlier, and I know I have to stop allowing myself to become so upset over things I have no control over. I didn't hear from Keisha all day and I can't say or write rather that, "That's okay." Because it's not. I still plan to do something about this situation because it's not pleasing. I have no complaints. I'm just going to turn in for the night and go back to work tomorrow. I'm thankful to God on this day for all that I have. I was just thinking while walking home from Stater Brother's about the choices I've made thus far in my life.

See I chose to get with Destiny even though after a few situations that occurred and I let it slide; kissing Mufu, kissing Rico at the beach when I drove her there, walking with Montel and holding his hand when she rode with me to Reseda's homecoming. I chose to allow myself to get her pregnant. I chose to move back to San Bernardino. I chose to put my hands on her back in 1992, and I chose to move out and leave her and the children. I chose to marry Keisha not even knowing her. I chose to continue to be with her after she cheated on me, then I chose to cheat on her. I chose to tell her to leave with the car. I chose to have unprotected sex. I chose to continue to drink and smoke. All of these choices have seriously affected my life tremendously and were unwise decisions. Even though it's said that, "Everything works according to God's will." I chose, I chose, I chose.

"You gotta be bad, you gotta be bold,
you gotta be wiser
You gotta be hard, you gotta be
tough, you gotta be stronger
You gotta be cool, you gotta be
calm, you gotta stay together
All I know, all I know, love will save
the day
Herald what your mother said
Read the books your father read
Try to solve the puzzles in your own
sweet time
Some may have more cash than
you
take a different view
My oh my
Time asks no questions, it goes on
without you
Leaving you behind if you can't
stand the pace
The world keeps on spinning
Can't stop it if you tried to
The best part is danger staring you
in the face, oh
Remember, listen as your day
unfolds
Challenge what the future holds
Try and keep your head up to the
sky
Lovers, they may cause you tears
Go ahead release your fears."
-Des'ree

Journal insert

27NOV1999: I'm always waiting, at least it seems like it. I was supposed to go to the Catch Club in Los Angeles with Renee tonight. I called her on her cell phone, and she was already in Los Angeles. She said she wasn't going to the club because her hair wasn't done. My question is, when was she going to call and tell me?! We made plans to go to this club, which is a gay club, that I went to with Lewis earlier this year. Jennifer just called so I'll write later because I also need to write about an accident with Kirk, my homeboy I met while attending San Bernardino Valley College, that happened on Monday.

Journal insert

28NOV1999: I just got in from TGI Friday's. I went with Valerie and her three kids, her brother, and Alan. Blue called me earlier and I was supposed to go out with him. He never called back or came through; another FLAKE. Anyway, I didn't have the greatest time, but it was alright. On to the story about Kirk. I called Kirk earlier today and he told me that him and his cousin Kem was in a car accident Monday night around 9:45 p.m. after leaving work. He said that he was stopped at a red light listening to the radio with his windows up. The next thing he remembered was waking up in an ambulance. He later found out that a guy got shot in the head and ran into the back of his car. Kirk suffered a broken wrist and had to have a few stitches on his forehead from his head hitting the stirring wheel and breaking his eye glasses. He told me that the suspects knew the victim and that the victim was a white man and was dating a black woman.

The only thing that I could come to is that the suspects were related to the woman or one of them used to date her. Regardless, it was a terrible thing to do. When the suspects shot the victim, the bullet went through his head and bounced around and hit the passenger in the leg. One act of ignorance caused problems in four lives: the passenger, Kirk, Kem, and the victim. May God rest his soul. I'm just amazed how one minute Kirk was sitting at the stop light after leaving work minding his own business and the next thing ya know, he's in the ambulance bleeding with a broken wrist, needing stitches, and without a car because his car got totaled. The authorities had to tear the car open to get Kem out. All and all thank God Kirk is still alive and able.

Journal insert

29NOV1999: Keisha paged me at 7:29 p.m. I paged her back and left a voice message that I wasn't home and that I would call her when I got home. I got home about 9:00 p.m. I called her apartment about a quarter to ten. She wasn't home so I left a message that I was returning her page. She never called back. I had a long conversation with Valerie: real deep. I told her that I wanted to kiss her Saturday night. She told me that she knew that. I REALLY did want to kiss her. I guess I was turned on by her legs because she had on some shorts and a tight little t-shirt that read, "Players." I already told her I know she's a player. Our conversation was deep last night. She made some valid points about how I need to fix my current situation. That she doesn't want to be just another female passing through my life, and if we had sex right now, we would lose respect for each other. Like I said, she brought up some valid points.

Val also made a statement about me smoking and drinking. She saw me outside of TGI Friday's smoking. I didn't know she was going to come outside also but she did. Boy I'm lucky that I didn't do something that I thought about doing. Soon as we all walked into Friday's, three young black, obviously gay to me, guys were walking out. When I walked back out to smoke my cigarette, they were at their car bumpin some music. I thought about going over to their car and asking them, "Where the party at?" It's a good thing I didn't because I wasn't outside for five minutes before Valerie came out behind me. This week, I'm going to try not to think about men or women other than my wife. I'm going to try to keep my mouth shut if I don't have anything good to say. I'm going to read my bible more this week. I already told myself I can't drink during the work week because I have to get up too early. I'm going to tell myself that I'm not going to buy packs of cigarettes this week. Maybe one or two singles from the doughnut shop but no more than two a day at least this week.

*This week Monday 29th - Saturday 4th 1999
No drinking the night before work
No more than two cigarettes a day
No sex unless it's with my wife Keisha

Journal insert

02DEC1999: I'm sitting at the bus stop downtown on my way to the gym. So far, this week I've stuck to my plan of not drinking the night before work, smoking only two cigarettes a day, and I have not had sex with anyone except Keisha; and not even jacked off. The last person I had sex with was Maxine on Thanks-For-Giving-Us your land day morning. I had other things that I was planning on controlling myself with this week also that I didn't write down because I think the bus came. This week I've really been trying not to speak negatively about anyone and try to say nothing if I had nothing positive or nice to say. I talked to Renee yesterday. Even though it's really hard to say anything positive about her after finding out she lied to me Saturday about going out. I called her yesterday at work to ask her if I could pay her that C-note I owe her on the 10th of December. She said it was cool like that. We talked more and she told me that she loved me. I said (I think I said), "Is that right?"

Then I asked her if she had fun at the club Saturday. She asked, "Who told you I went to the club?" I told her don't worry about all of that. I asked her again; did she have fun. She said she didn't go. I said, "A minute ago you just told me you loved me and now you're lying to me?" Then she asked, "Who told you that I was at the club?" Anyway, my point is she LIED!! I don't know but I think I'm offended about that. I was telling Valerie about that situation, and she doesn't really think that it was that big of a deal. To me it is. First of all, it tells me that I can't really believe what Renee tells me. Even though we've been "FRIENDS" (with benefits) for a long time, I don't think I could take her word at face value anymore. I already knew she was a cheater now a LIAR. Next, I guess a thief. I don't know. I know I'm not perfect myself, but I promise you that I try not to lie to people, especially my so-called friends and loved ones. Now when I write I try not to. That doesn't mean that I lie for my convenience or anyone else. Sometimes I may be lying and really honestly not be aware of it. I know in order for my conscience to be clear with myself and God, I'm going to tell the truth so help me God, and if I feel like I'm backed into a corner, I'll plead the FIFTH!!

On to something else. Violet has been taking a dance class at Valley College. She told me a while ago that she would be in a dance recital. I totally forgot until I came home today from getting my hair done, it looks cool. I need to work some gel in it. I listened to my messages. I really don't like how Violet reminded me the day of the event! Anyway, I had to work. I was going to try and get Destiny to pick me up at 7:30 p.m., but when I asked if Lucas was going and she said, "Probably." I told her that I wasn't going to go because I didn't have a ride. Wilson Philips *Hold On* is playing on 9.27 FM. I love this song!!! I just love positive motivating songs. They inspire me! Alan just called. He's coming over to spend the night. Anyway, I told Destiny that I wasn't going. She asked if I was going to ride with Rose.

I explained to her that I'm not asking Rose for a ride or to use her car anymore. I should have known that wasn't going to last long. I called Keisha to see if she wanted to go. She told me she had plans to go to dinner and to see *The Nutcracker* with the school, the school she works for. I should have asked her who she went to dinner with. Like that really matters. I'm going to smoke a cigarette before Alan gets here. I've already drank half a beer. I'll write later.

Well, I'm back. That was my third cigarette today. I know I said two a day this week, but I did not promise because I can't do promises, not at this time in my life. I don't feel bad because I am trying and I'm going to keep trying. I'm a little horny but I'm more tired. This beer is affecting me. I can tell by how I'm writing but I don't have to work tomorrow. I'm not scheduled but I might try to go in anyway because I need the money. I don't know what God has planned for me, but I hope it's something wonderful. I'm learning more and more, and I think I am becoming calmer as I wait and work. I've been up since 2:00 a.m. because I had to be at Pic n Save at 3:00 a.m. I worked there for six hours and then got my hair done. I then went to Smart and Final for six hours. I'm tired and I'm tired. Alan hasn't got here yet, but I think I'm going to lay down now. I just feel that I'm in this fight to get myself on my feet by myself. God is with me because He's keeping me motivated. I just have to press on to the goal.

"Remember,
when you make promises
for tomorrow
also remember
that tomorrow
isn't
promised to you."
-Ignatius J 17DEC1999

Journal insert

11DEC1999: What's crackin lackin? I know I haven't written in a few days. I've been very busy working my ass off and trying to avoid bullshit. I've really been sticking to basically two cigarettes a day. I think it's only been a couple of days when I had two. I haven't been drinking on days when I had to work the next day. That's been all week because I've been working straight since, I believe November 29th, that's 13 days straight!! I had a beer last Friday night, but I didn't know that I was going to work that Saturday. That Saturday morning, Marion, my boss at Pic n Save, called me in. Well, I'm drinking a beer now because I don't have to work tomorrow. I'm still hyped and motivated so hopefully I'll put in 70 hours next week from working both jobs like I just about did this week. I think about 27 at Smart and Final and 38 at Pic n Save. I really want a car!!

I was going to buy a Ford Taurus from this guy I met at The Elks Club, but everybody has basically warned me not to mess with Ford Taurus's because they are bad cars. I'll let that be my last resort. I have to keep working hard for this money because if I can get a car, more opportunities will be opened for me. I haven't had sex or masturbated in over two weeks. I know that's not really a long time but for me at this period in my life that's a little something. I'm human so I do have my urges, but I have to exercise some kind of discipline. Hoes are fuckin silly to me anyway. Well excuse me, women. They just trip me out. I just got off the phone with Valerie.

Journal insert

16DEC1999: I'm laying here frustrated! Today a few things really got under my skin and bugged me. First, I was attempting to get a car from Cars 4 Less where Keisha and I got the Toyota Corolla from. Barbara took me there Tuesday and I filled out another application. They told me it would be a few hours. So, Barbara and I went to a few other places looking at cars. Then we went to lunch at Cajun Garden. When I got to Smart and Final, I called Cars 4 Less about 4:30 p.m. Louis, an employee, told me that the finance company wouldn't approve me for a $5000 car. I told him to try for a $2000 car. He told me he would. I called back yesterday, and Louis was said to be out until Friday. Another employee began to check things out for me. She told me to call back Thursday afternoon and she would have something back from the credit report. I called this morning from Pic n Save and she told me to call around 2:00 p.m.

Barbara picked me up at 11:00 a.m. so we went and got some Chinese food and went and checked on the Ford Taurus. Ol boy told me he sold it Saturday after lying at first about not having one for sale. He offered me a Ford Tempo which I didn't like, and it smelled like someone pissed in it!! Barbara and I went to Cars 4 Less. As soon as I walked on the lot, I saw a Honda Accord for $2977 and a few other decent cars for the same amount. Ol boy didn't know who I was and I told him I was interested in one of the cars in the range of $2977. He told me he had not received my credit report back approving me. I told him that it shouldn't be that hard getting me into a car with $800 down for a car in that range. He told me that he would not except $400 this week and

$400 next week. That he would want $1000 up front AND my credit was terrible and that my wife basically got the car because of her credit.

Now what kind of shit is that? She wasn't even working when we got that car. I was working both jobs and Louis told us in about a year we could upgrade or finance another car. I do believe that is what he said! **Little did I realize, while attending Rosston Security College, that I had taken out a loan to pay for it. At just 18 years old, I signed a legal contract that began the downfall of my credit. I was young and dumb, clueless about contracts, loans, repayments, or deferments. Even now, I'll admit I'm still a bit ignorant when it comes to contracts and credit.**

The other thing that frustrated me today is I went to Bible study last night and I talked to Brother Cooper. He told me that Keisha and I could not divorce because we were both out doing wrong: FUCKING! I paged her today and called her. She is still seeing some dude she met at the club. She told me she talked to Abdul, and he told her I said we're going to get a divorce. I confirmed that with her. She asked me if I had been fucking and I told her, "No." Which I haven't in three weeks now!! I know she's been fucking around because she told me. I have grounds for divorce and that's what I'm going to do. I'll probably talk to Brother Cooper tomorrow at Youth Night. I'm going to let her go. I'm not going to trip because all these whores that I've fucked around with got people in their lives even my own fuckin WIFE!!! Can you believe that SHIT!! Look at the FUCKIN LOSERS they have settled for!!! Keisha silly ass just met this dude at a club.

Then again, I think she told me she knew him from back in the day. REGARDLESS, FUCK EM ALL!!!

The third thing that frustrated me today is that I bought some tools to switch the refrigerator door so it would be easier to open. I was able to unscrew the top, but I couldn't unscrew the bottom. I'm about to call Destiny and talk to her for a minute. Then I'm going to try to go to work for a few hours at Smart and Final because I was off there today. I told Barbara since I can't sin like I used to, I may as well become a workaholic! I'm still going to get a car. I'll just have to save my money!!

Journal insert

22DEC1999: I'm not going to write much even though I have a lot on my mind. I just got off from Smart and Final at 7:00 p.m. I've worked 14 hours today. From 4:00 a.m., I worked six hours at Pic n Save and eight hours at Smart and Final. My time at Smart and Final feels limited. There's so much crap that seems to be going on and a lot that I'm not at all pleased with. God knows my heart. I'll continue to pray about the things that are bothering me. On the way home I ran across Mickey. He was waiting for me. He is terrible. He wouldn't leave unless I kissed him. We were outside of my apartments because I wouldn't let him come up. I kissed him after talking for a few minutes. The devil is busy. I still haven't had sex, and I'll continue to pray and stay away from fornication and masturbation. I have to stop writing now so I can get a little sleep. I have to be at Pic n Save at 12:00 a.m. I hope all this hard work pays off!! God bless me and keep me in Your will.

Journal insert

26DEC1999: What's up? Well, it's the day after Christmas, a man-made traditional holiday. Anyway, yesterday I went by Destiny's house to drop off Tomia and my goddaughter Precious's gifts. Precious was sleeping and Tomia was at Aunt Patricia's apartment. I had Rose's car, so I went to Aunt Pat's place. Tomia was happy to see me. I gave her her gifts and kicked it over there for a minute. Leah fixed me a plate. Barbara met me over there and I followed her to Sister Angela's, one of the sisters from church, apartment. I finally sat down and ate. I didn't want to sit and eat at Des's house because her and Lucas had a gang of company, seriously a gang. Not for real but they did look thuggish. Des hooked me up with a lot of food and desserts.

At Sister Angela's, I ate a fat plate that Barbara fixed for me. Sister Angela can cook cook that's FO SHO! Maxine paged me and left a voice message. I paged her back and told her to meet me at my apartment about 10:30 p.m. I left Sister Angela's about 10:25 p.m. When I got home, Rose was watching *Malcolm X*. Maxine hadn't called or showed up. I got undressed and laid down. Then Davis came over, then Maxine. Maxine and Rose went to the store and Davis left. I dossed off. Rose and Maxine came back but I was tired and didn't want to get up. They were up talking and watching a movie. Maxine spent the night. We didn't do anything, of course. Mainly because Rose was sleeping in the same room. Also, because I'm trying to not have sex. This morning, she asked me to take a shower with her and I told her, "No." The other night she called me about 1:00 a.m. and asked if she could come over and I told her, "No." Rose wasn't home that night; she was at the Metro Club in Riverside on a date.

This morning, Abdul called because I was supposed to go by his apartment yesterday. He told me that Keisha totaled the Toyota Corolla. I told him that's on her. She has insurance. She has to realize that God doesn't like ugly. If she's still fucking around that's on her also. Hopefully I'll see her at church tonight but if I don't then I won't. I'll probably page her. I have to pick up Alan from the bus station. He wants to go to the movies. I'm going to run by Abdul's apartment for a minute, only for a minute because Alan don't like Abdul. Anyway, it's time for me to roll cause Rose just got back.

Journal insert

31DEC1999: Well, it's the last day ... of the nineteen hundreds!!!!!! I had to stop writing for about two hours because Rose came in with Tiffany and Brandy. They went to Riverside to a house party. Now again I'm home alone drunk or I guess buzzed listening to Biggie's CD *Born Again*. I just got off the phone with Valerie. She's supposed to be coming through to pick me up later, but I tell you what, if she comes after 12 midnight, she cannot come. 12 midnight is the start of something totally, definitely, truly, undoubtedly brand new. It's the millennium!!! It's got to be the start of something perfectly new, something smoothly different, something obviously super unique. I am so buzzed I can barely concentrate. I really haven't eaten anything, I'm faded, I guess I'll smoke a cigarette. Things, of course, haven't been going according to the way I planned; life is just so complex to me.

I really don't know how I got to this point in my life, but I guess truly I do. I decided this I guess a long, long, long time ago. I'm all by myself. I told Alan recently that I don't think I will live a long life. Maybe my mark will be the first person to die in the year of 2000 in Southern California. I don't know, man, I'm just faded and maybe I'm just not fuckin too thrilled with the fuckin way that things are going in my fuckin life!!! Who's truly in control of this life I live!!! What's going on? How come happiness seems to be light years away? What's the deally yo!!!!!! 10:15 p.m. 12/31/99 - I don't like my life thus far, now what?

CHAPTER VI

Y2K

— · ◦ ● · · —

Journal insert

05JAN2000: I'm sitting here drinking a beer and just finished a cigarette. I'm about to go masturbate with my favorite toy! I guess I just enjoy anal sex. I just guess I like having a big dick in my ass hole even if it's artificial. I guess a so-called "man" has to do what he has to do. Things truly are not that great in my life right now. I've been angry, frustrated, tired mentally and physically, and depressed lately. Would a brand new 2000 convertible Mustang make all my woes go away? I don't think so, but it would be a start. I'm still working both jobs and I haven't got a car yet. I was attempting to save some money, but I got caught up in man's tradition "Christmas". Now I have to start over. And now I'm thinking about getting the cable turned back on. I think it's been off for about two months and some change. I can't discipline myself to read and stick to some type of schedule. My smoking habits picked up again and so have my masturbating habits. I fucked Maxine about a week or so ago and I'm willing to do it again.

I called Keisha earlier today to see if she would pick me up for Bible study tonight. She said she would call me and let me know but the bitch never called me back. She's rolling around in a new rental car because somebody ran into the back of the Corolla and totaled it. So now she's waiting on the insurance to kick in. Moms haven't heard from her lawyer in about four months from what my brother tells me. The accident has been almost a year now and she hasn't gotten shit! My cousin Marvin was in a car accident also and he has at least received a few grand from my understanding. Maybe she hasn't received anything because of me. Because of the things I would do with whatever she gives me. Because I would be a wild child. It's just not fair. For New Years Eve I stayed home alone, drank, and masturbated. I didn't want to get out of bed. Maybe I just need to stop depending on God so much and go out and get the things I want!!!! If I feel that not having a car got me fucked then I need to go get one!

2000! What's up now?!!!?

Journal insert

20JAN2000: The last time I wrote, I wrote, "2000! What's up now?!!!?". Well, nothing has been really up since I last wrote. I've masturbated three times since I've last written and that includes the day that I wrote. Twice with my favorite toy and once just jacking off. I fucked Maxine once since I last wrote. I was supposed to spend the night at her dad's house with her while he's out of town. Her so-called Ex-Boyfriend kept calling. I just told her to take me home cuz I wasn't feeling too comfortable. Mickey popped up at my apartment while Rose was here. I talked to him outside on the balcony. He wanted to talk to me in his brand-new BMW. We went and sat inside of his car with the air conditioner running and talked for a bit. I swear there's nothing like the smell of a brand-new car. Of course, after the small talk he wanted me to suck his dick. I was reluctant and Mickey being Mickey he persisted. He said that he would drive to the side of the law firm building at the end of my block. I told him to go ahead and drive down the block.

So, Mickey drove down the street and parked in a secluded shaded area in the law firm's parking lot. Mickey being Mickey, of course his dick was already out. I leaned down and began sucking his already erect and hungry dick. Even though I was reluctant at first, I enjoyed sucking Mickey's dick probably just as much as he enjoyed having me suck it. The sloppy toppy got good to the both of us until he tightly grabbed my head with both of his hands and told me he was cumming. He wanted to cum in my mouth and I told him, "No." I finished him up by jacking his creamy warm nutt out of his pulsating rock-hard dick onto his shirt as some of it unexpectedly shot onto my lips. I looked up at him into his beautiful soft brown eyes and licked his sweet nutrients off my lips and then I wiped him up. We kissed passionately as we always do, and he drove me back to my apartment.

A few hours later, I went to church service. I know I have deep-rooted unresolved issues. Sometimes I just don't know what to do! Sometimes I feel like I'm too hard on myself and most of the times I don't think I'm hard enough. I'm about to read my bible when I finish writing because that's what I started off doing. But I decided to write and catch up on things. I cooked dinner because I told Rose last night that I would. She started a new job Monday and plus she's been going to school at night. To me she's been doing pretty good and once again all praise to God. I prayed hard for Rose.

I really can't have wishy washy faith. I have prayed for a lot of things and God came through for me and the people I've prayed for. The devil is very tricky and will and has tempted me to think that the things that occur are coincidences. I have to pray for strength in that area. I'm going to start my reading and hopefully I can apply what I read to my life. I have so much bottled up in me right now. Sexuality, marriage, my relationship with Tomia, not having a car, a good woman, smoking cigarettes, wanting to smoke some wacky tobacky, drinking, worldly pressures, just everything. Aunt Darlene committed herself into rehab on New Year's Day. I hope she gets better, and I also hope that's not what it's going to take for me to get it together. **Wishful thinking. Rehab is exactly what it took to finally get me off the bottle after about 30 years of drinking.** I want to write out a list of the things I want to do but most of it conflicts with the will of God from my understanding.

Journal insert

21FEB2000: Damn it's been almost a month since I wrote. I know I haven't been as dedicated lately to anything. I haven't been to the gym in a while either. I'm a little buzzed from three shots of tequila. I probably didn't spell that right, but I accept that. There are a few things that I'm not good at and I must accept that. At the same time, I must accept and appreciate the things that I am good at. Lately nothing really has happened in my life. February 1st, I decided that I wasn't going to drink or smoke but that originally supposed to have been for 21 days. Then I decided to do it for 29 days because February only has 29 days this month. I failed on February 11th. I drank and I masturbated with my favorite toy. AND again on the 13th AND on the 17th I smoked. The 19th - all the above. Tonight, drinking and one cigarette so far. I'm not going to write much else because I'm faded, and Valerie is supposed to be coming over. Hopefully she'll let me fuck. Jennifer just called. We didn't talk too much or too long. I don't know where I'm headed, I really don't. I guess I'm headed to the kitchen to cook some fries to go with my hot wings.

Journal insert

23FEB2000: Valerie came by, and we talked (deeply) about a lot of things. I told her about the episode of *Alley McBeal* I had seen. It was basically about a guy that wanted to date Alley. She worked in his coffee shop with him because she had to do community service. They had a great time working together. Afterwards as he walked her to her apartment, he leaned in to kiss her, but she stuck her hand out to shake his hand. But he kissed her anyway. Then he told her that he's bisexual and he wanted her to know up front because he wanted to date her. She didn't want to date him. It really was a good episode. I guess I enjoyed it so much because I can relate to it. I didn't tell Valerie the part that I can relate to though. She asked me if I was bisexual. I basically told her that I have had relations with men in the past. I really don't know what I classify myself as being. I guess I classify myself as being married because that's what I am. Keisha called me and then she said she would call me back.

When she did call back, I unplugged the phone because Valerie was here. A couple of weeks ago, I asked the church to pray for Keisha and I. When I went to Mt. View Church, Brother Bell, the preacher, told me that he would pray for us also. I know that prayer changes things. When Keisha called me, maybe that could have been the beginning of something new and promising. But she irritated me when she first called. I asked, "Who is this?" She said, "Keisha." I said, "Oh, what's up?" She responded, "There you go!" What the fuck do she mean, "There you go?" There I go WHAT??!! I just don't know. I've been reluctant to call her. I've been thinking about her a lot. I don't think I can be myself with her. I don't want to lie to her. Hell, I really don't know who I am or what I want and adding her or anyone to my life right now would only complicate it MORE!!!

Journal insert

29FEB2000: I went up to Keisha's job. She had been on my mind for a while. Plus, this marriage being in limbo has been frustrating me. So, I wanted to try to reconcile things with my wife. She came outside of the school, and we talked out in front. Then Brother Cooper drove by and saw us and turned around. We talked with him for a few minutes and then he left because he was in a hurry. Keisha told me my hair looked nice (which blew me away coming from her). She talked about her job for a few minutes. I told her basically that I wanted us to talk to somebody, either Brother Cooper or Brother Bell from the Mt. View Church.

I understood that she was interested; I understood wrong. Friday I had flowers sent to her job with a note saying: "I hope that our past will be a learning experience, I hope our present will be a healing experience, and I hope that our future will be a heavenly experience." All Friday I didn't hear from her. Saturday, while at work at Pic n Save, I called her and paged her. I even called Brother Cooper twice to hook up a meeting with him for Keisha and I. I found out he had gone with his wife to a marriage seminar.

Sunday, I got up bright and early and cooked breakfast for me and Tomia. I got ready for church and called my loving wife Keisha to see if she would come to church and hopefully talk to Brother Cooper with me about what we intend to do about our marriage. She never called or paged me back with an answer just like Saturday. After service, I came home and called her apartment. I asked her if she wanted to talk to Brother Cooper with me. She said that she already told him that she didn't want to work out our marriage. I was trying to tell her that my main focus was for us both to talk with him so that he would be a witness to what we decided to do. She put me on hold. In about two minutes of waiting, I hung up.

A minute later my phone rang, I answered. It was her boyfriend Red. **Red was a thug — like a dirty red bone, tatted, skinny dude with braids. He kinda reminded me of Bizzy Bone from Bone Thugs n Harmony, just dirty.** He told me not to call Keisha anymore. I said alright and hung the phone up. Then I went back to church. When evening service was over, I informed Brother Cooper of what happened. He called for Brother Singer to be a witness to our conversation. They both advised me that the ball is in my court if I have not been sleeping around. Which I haven't been for about a month, which is what I told them. Brother Cooper told me to be patient and so did Brother Singer. He told me I should fast and pray. Brother Cooper told me that he would call Keisha. After I left the church, I went to kick it with Davis and Latoya.

When I got home, my brother told me that some dude called the apartment and thought he was me. He told him pretty much some bullshit concerning Keisha. Jesse called me when I was in the bathroom praying. I told him what was going on and he told me I gave Keisha enough chances, and to leave her before someone gets hurt. He's right. I believe that I have tried enough. Dirty Red can have her. I'm just trying to get my life in order now. I need a serious vacation, I really do. When I got in last night, Brother Noah had called me, Rose said. I called him back because I knew it was concerning my wife. He wanted to counsel us. I told him to just forget it because it's over. I informed him that I would call Brother Cooper and ask him not to call her.

That's why I think Dusty Red called back to my apartment Sunday evening. I think after I finished talking to Brother Cooper he called Keisha. All of this is getting squashed this week. Keisha and I will be divorced. I forgive her for all the crap we've been through, but I don't forgive her enough to accept her back as my wife. It's over. Now I'm on my way back home because if I continue on to the gym, I wouldn't have time to work out. I'm not pissed or upset. All things happen for a reason or reasons that we humans may never understand. I'll try to go again tomorrow morning and if not, the next morning. I'll keep trying and I will piece my life back together. I'm going to start going to Bible study every Wednesday night, bible video classes every Thursday night, worship service every Sunday morning and evening. I'm going to get on track and get my life together. I have to.

Journal insert

04MAR2000: Well, as I wrote, everything happens for reasons that may be far beyond human understanding. When I returned home from my vain attempt to go to the gym, I laid down and watched television. I dozed off briefly. Then there was a knock at the door. It was a little after 11:00 a.m. and I couldn't think of anyone it could be. So, I went to the door, and it was Delinquent Red (Keisha's boyfriend). Can you believe that!?! He gave me a summons for divorce court! Keisha sent him! Just unbelievable! But all things, yeah, ya know.

I went to Bible study Wednesday night at church. I really wanted to go to ask the church for prayers for Keisha and because we were still having problems. I basically told the congregation that I was going to need their prayers and soon I would disclose the situation to them. Brother Cooper felt that the congregation should know right then what exactly I needed prayers for. He told the congregation that I was planning on divorcing Keisha because she has someone (a man) living with her and she refuses to reconcile.

So, according to Matthew, I have book, chapter, and verse to divorce her. I wasn't too comfortable with him doing that and after talking to Barbara, I was really uncomfortable. But now I'm moving on. It's just that Brother Cooper doesn't realize how Keisha is. I believe she would come up to the church (if she found out what Brother Cooper announced) and tell everyone about the affairs I had in the past or she could just trip.

The whole fact is we didn't know each other when we got married. Two wolves in sheep's clothing are what Keisha and I were. We had major disagreements, she cheated, I cheated, she read my journals without my consent, she couldn't and wouldn't accept my past and instead ridiculed me about it. We could no longer live peacefully with each other. I asked

her to leave. I told her to leave with the car.

She left with someone she was seeing. I stayed in my apartment because I acquired it before I met her. I continued seeing Brenda, June, Maxine and Mickey. I moved from the two bedrooms into a studio apartment closer to my job because I no longer had transportation. Keisha tried to move in but wouldn't stop going out. I asked her to leave, and she did. I've been celibate for a little over a month. Keisha is still with the person she's been with. She refuses to reconcile. I just heard a noise at my window. Now I don't know if it was someone out there messing with my window or God warning me about what I was going to write. Come to find out, it was a cat on my air conditioner. See what alcohol and bud will do? Make ya all paranoid and stuff. I'll finish later.

Journal insert

12MAR2000: I didn't get up and go to church this morning. I didn't want to call Barbara for a ride and plus Jennifer came over last night. She picked me up from work at Pic n Save. We stopped by Stater Brother's and she bought me some more food.

Afterwards, we kicked it at my crib, smoked some bud, and I drank a beer. She fixed me something to eat. We watched Janet Jackson's *Red Velvet Rope* concert. I could tell she wanted to fuck. I can't go there with her anymore. Especially right now!! I haven't had sex since January 31st! I cannot until my divorce is final! Hopefully I won't have sex after the divorce and not until I marry again. Right now, I have to take it one thing at a time! After Jennifer left, I went in the bathroom and masturbated with my favorite toy. I paged Renee today and left a message on her home phone. She hasn't called me back yet. She probably won't. I know I won't hold my breath on it.

Val (Valerie) came into Pic n Save last night buying some thongs and cucci shorts. I told her to bring it over. She never showed up. Last Saturday I called Allison. We went out to dinner, my treat. She told me she was going to cook the next day. I told her that I wanted to come over. I haven't heard from her since. Jesse told me Wednesday that he would be out here Saturday. He did not call or show up! I don't know why there are sooooo many FLAKES in my life. Maybe God is showing me I can only count on HIM or maybe I need to take care of my own happiness. Jennifer would be at my beck and call for ANYTHING and EVERYTHING!!! She's 50 years old and I'm 29. That's a 21-year difference AND she has eight children!!

I am not attracted to her sexually at all. For 50 she looks 65. I'll just leave it at that because I don't want to disrespect her in any way. She is a beautiful giving friend that I am grateful to have. **I've been in two relationships with significant age gaps. Naomi was 21, and I was 32 when we got together —an 11-year gap.**

Then there was Raphael; he was 20, and I was 36 —making it a 16-year gap. The thing is —and I'm NOT being conceded —I was FINE! I was in good shape, had a nice body, and was working. Honestly, I'm still more attracted and drawn to individuals younger than me. I swear, people my age look twice as old! They look worn out, overweight, and just seem slow. Meanwhile, I love working out, looking good, feeling good, traveling, and experiencing new things. Where could a relationship with Jennifer go? Nowhere beyond friendship.

I applied for two new credit cards. Lately I've been thinking heavily about the Army!! I told Jennifer last night, "Life doesn't change unless you change your routine. Changing your routine gradually changes your life gradually. Changing your life dramatically changes your life DRAMATICALLY!!" You have no way of knowing if that dramatic change would be for the best or worse. I think that I have a long list of good reasons to go. I can't really give one good reason not to. So now, what am I waiting on?!

Journal insert

16MAR2000: I guess I have ONE very good reason not to go into the Army. If I have to lie to get in, then I'm not going! Davis's girlfriend Latoya brought that to my attention the other night. That is so real to me. Every thought should be like that. If I have to lie about it, then it's not for me!! **That did not stick long AT ALL!!**

Right now, I'm chillin alone listening to Shania Twain's *Come On Over* CD, smoking a little bud I got from Jennifer, and taking shots of Tequila. I've had three so far. I'm a little buzzed. I am going to look through my newly purchased, "Black Inches Magazine".

Keisha paged me last night to tell me her boyfriend got arrested. She told me this morning when I called her job. She called me tonight, then she put me on hold for too long, so I hung up. I need to talk to her. I need to know where her head is because I'm tired of being in limbo! I haven't had sex in almost two months. The last time she had sex was probably the night before ol boy went to jail. The last time Destiny probably fucked Lucas was this morning. Renee and her girlfriend are probably getting it on right now. I have to realize they were all in sin. Even though I have sex with myself, from my understanding it's an act of sexual immorality, but it is not the worse sin against the body like fornication is. I still have issues. All sin is bad from my understanding. There are different consequences for various sins. Some consequences are greater than others depending on the sin. I do not know if that is true or not. I have to study more.

Journal insert

26MAR2000: I am only going to write briefly because I'm high and buzzed off some Ole English beer. Jennifer came over and we smoked some bud. I'm high and was higher. I almost landed on the planet insanity. I started thinking too deep and getting paranoid. I talked to God (prayed). I told HIM that I want to do right, which I do, and I want to do what HE wants me to do. It was something like that. I know I want to do right and to me that's doing the will of God. I still haven't had sex and it's going on two months. I can't allow myself to have any sexual relations with anyone other than my wife in order to divorce the "correct way" in the sight of God. Keisha's boyfriend has been in jail for about two or three weeks now. I heard from Keisha maybe twice. She hasn't been to church. She doesn't want me. If she did, she would come to me. Then again, it could be me being stubborn and ego trippin. I'm going to call her after my Ginuwine CD stops playing. I'm going to tell her or ask her if she wants to be with me regardless of my past and shortcomings. If she does, then we're going to work this marriage out in God's name. If she doesn't agree then I'll have to let her go! PERIODT! BLANK!

Journal insert

30MAR2000: What's up? I'm chillin listening to my R Kelly CD. I just had a beer. There's still some left in the refrigerator. Starting Sunday, I will attempt to stop smoking and drinking so much. I have to realize that I reap what I sow, the bible teaches that. Tomorrow will be another 40 hours of work at the Fontana Smart and Final. I thank God! Rent is paid tomorrow and if it's in God's will, I will put $400 down on a Nissan 300zx. I found one for sale for $1200. I hope it is in God's will. I am not going to force it. Either it works out or it doesn't; the money still will be for a car. I'm going to roll in April. During the Fontana project, I learned that there is another remodel project coming up next week, a four-week project. My old assistant manager is in charge of the remodel. I've talked to him about helping with the remodel. I told him I would stay with my aunt in Los Angeles so I would be closer. I talked to Aunt Lois and asked her if I would be able to stay with her. She said it would be fine. Rose will be moving this weekend: Saturday! I love her. I've accepted her as my family, as my daughter has, but she has to go! I'm tired of people using me to get where they need to go. Stepping on me to reach whatever needs to be reached in their life. When she moves, I cannot allow anyone except my wife to move in with me.

My wife cannot move in unless she promises to be a WIFE!! I've written it in my heart that my 30's would be the best years; better yet, the beginning of the best years of my life! It's just time for changes. Time to move forward. Time to make things happen. My hair is growing. I've gotten a couple of more piercings; my nipple and tongue. Hopefully in God's will, I'll get this car and decorate my apartment with new furniture. Maybe hopefully if God will, I'll get on the merchandising team with Smart and Final! 40 hours a week and $16.10 an hour and I'll get to travel to different stores. I don't know what's best for me. I think I know what I need, but God knows exactly what I need! I do know I've been thinking about preaching lately. I want to preach my sermon on May 7, 2000. It'll be exactly one year after granny passed away. May the Lord wrap her soul in eternal peace!!! I don't care what any religion says, that's what I hope!

Journal insert

22APR2000: I'm chillin here buzzed off some bud and I ain't talking about Bud Light. Sipping on some Jack Daniels on the rocks at home alone. I really don't have any complaints. I've been working a lot of hours! About 40 hours a week for about four weeks straight. It started when I went to work at the Fontana Smart and Final. The company was moving the store to a new location in

Fontana. I worked there for two weeks and then went back to the San Bernardino Smart and Final, my home store, and the hours were good. The next week my hours dropped to 28 but it's better than 15 hours!! Yesterday I had $500 in my savings account. My bills, household bills, are taken care of. I paid that $41 water bill that I've been owing since I lived on D Street. I just want to take care of my obligations, the things I started. I'm really hoping I get a car before July because I want to drive to Tennessee. I want to meet my mother out there. I also want to take Violet and Tomia with me. That's just the beginning of my near cited goals.

Journal insert

23 APR 2000: Well, it's "East Star" or Easter. Abdul just left about 10 minutes ago. He came over this morning to take me to church. I couldn't find anything to wear. So, we kicked it, watched *Double Jeopardy*, and got high. He wanted to see the Lakers game at 12:00 p.m. I told him I would go with him, and he told me to find who was watching it. So, I called Aunt Pat to see if Rashad was watching it. She said he was lying down because he didn't feel good. I got up and started ironing my shirt after putting my pants and shoes on. Abdul came in the kitchen saying that he could see Kobe Bryant playing on the television but I know he wasn't talking about seeing him on my television because I don't have cable. Anyway, he was all in a hurry to leave. He said he would go watch the game in Banning. I just think it was fucked up because I was trying to hang out with him. He knows I don't have a car or any family I can kick it with. Maybe I just expect too much from friendships. Today did not become too lonely after all.

Rebecka, my neighbor called and wanted to come over and kick it. She came over, we watched *Double Jeopardy*, played a couple games of dominoes and a couple rounds of cards. She's cool people. I took her out once when I had Rose's car. I took her to see *Next Friday* at the Ontario Mills. It was a cool date. After she left, I took a nap. **I met Rebecka while I was working as a cashier at Smart and Final. She came through my line, and we sparked up a lil' convo. I thought she was pretty as hell, and it was clear she was diggin' me too. Rebecka was a little shorter than me, Mexican and white, with long dark hair that flowed down her back, green eyes, small breast (just the way I like 'em), and a nice, nice ass. Honestly, I would say she was my J. Lo, and I was her P. Diddy. She told me that I reminded her of the singer Joe.**

We discovered that we were neighbors, and as I mentioned in my journal entry above, she was cool people. The first time we chilled together started when she called me one afternoon asking what I was doing. I told her I was taking a bath —which I was. She then asked if she could come over and join me. I thought she was bullshittin', but I told her, "Fo sho." She surprised me by actually showing up and getting in the tub with me. That shit was so fly.

From that point, it was on like Donkey Kong. I loved being with her —fucking her and eating her pussy. She loved getting dicked down by me, too. She was so fucking soft and smelled like strawberries. I really wanted to boo her up, but she wasn't ready to take it there. I think she was still fucking around with her baby daddy. That was a bummer

because I really wanted her to be mine, even though I was still married and had not told her I fuck with dudes too.

Our encounters fizzled out after I got burnt and told her she needed to get checked out. I'm pretty sure I caught it from Toneka, but who knows —it could've been her. Either way, that was my first time catching an STD, and sadly, it wasn't my last.

Then Abdul came by. He's really been trippin me out lately. A couple of weeks ago I was doing my laundry, and I had on my hospital pants (scrubs) and I believe a tank top. He was walking behind me, and he asked me if I had on any underwear. And I told him, "No." I asked him why was he looking at my ass. One day we landed on the conversation about my dildo, and he asked if he could see it. I told him no and that that is personal. I did show him a gay magazine I bought, "Black Inches". I showed him my favorite models: Black Thunder, Dyke, and Mega Body. Today when he was over, we talked. I don't know how we got completely on the subject, but I know I made a comment to him after he told me to shut my mouth. I asked, "Why? If I don't, are you going to put something in it?" He replied, "Yeah, my dick." We then got on the subject of sucking dick.

I told him that I sucked Mickey's dick. I asked him if he had gotten his dick sucked while in jail and he told me no. He said he was going to fuck this one guy, but I can't recall why he didn't. I know we are skating on thin ice with God, ourselves and our so-called "friendship". Earlier today when I was sitting on the toilet (which I normally do in the nude and so does he from what he told me), he came in the bathroom and his eyes fell directly between my legs. Renee told me a while ago that Abdul wants to fuck me. More and more I believe it and sadly I want him to. It just can't be, not under these circumstances! Later Abdul and I returned from the video store. Jennifer pulled up. We all kicked it for a minute and Abdul had to leave. Jennifer and I smoked another joint. I've been drinking and smoking all day.

Journal insert

26MAY2000: I went to work from 2:00 p.m. until 10:30 p.m. We had to prep for inventory. I'm the new Freezer Supervisor so I had to prep the freezer. Major, my boss, wasn't happy with Richard's performance as the Freezer Supervisor, so he appointed me in charge of the freezer. After seven years with the company, I finally have a specific responsibility assigned to me. No raise though. I order the freezer loads, work the freezer loads, and prep the freezer. I thank God for all things.

Today after work I drank a beer. I haven't drunk a beer since Sunday and it's now Friday. I guess that is good considering that I had been drinking every day!! I smoked two cigarettes today and smoked a little weed. I hadn't smoked a cigarette since Tuesday and no weed since Sunday. I'm a little disappointed because I fasted for 24 hours and prayed about stopping these habits. I know I shouldn't expect to stop overnight. It just disturbs me. I'm thinking about fasting tomorrow for another 24 hours or maybe Saturday and Sunday. I just don't want to defile this temple God has allowed me to dwell in. I don't want to cause it to have cancer or cause it to have or develop liver failure. I am responsible for my actions. I have to get a grip. Even if that means getting help!!

That help didn't come until 18 years later. When I had reached my breaking point, alcohol had become my only friend. In March of 2018, I had been taken by ambulance to the emergency room four times due to alcohol abuse and depression. The "help" I so desperately needed finally came when I was admitted to 2 North East, the psychiatric and detox ward at Jerry L. Pettis Memorial Veteran's Hospital. Hours are back to normal. Thank God that doesn't mean 15 hours. I have 26 and that's decent. I'll have time to go to the gym and time to seek out counseling. Tomia is off track from school, so I'll spend a lot of time with her.

Anthony's, my assistant manager, wife is selling a car, an Infiniti. I told him that I am interested. He said he would talk to his wife and see if he can make me a deal. His wife's brother is supposed to be interested in the car also. The Lord's will will be done. Whomever he wants to have the car will have it. I'm going to pray on it and that's going to be that. I believe it will be mine. It was made clear to me that this is not the time to finance a car. I cannot allow myself to do that unless I'm full time and I believe that there is wisdom.

CHAPTER VII

What About Your - Friends - How Many of Us Have Them

Journal insert

05JUNE2000: What's up? Ain't nothing. I was going to say the same ol shit but it ain't! I have a new outlook on my so-called friends. First off, my "FRIEND" Davis got married yesterday. I was his best man. I called my "FRIEND" Kirk Saturday from the barbershop and asked him if he wanted to hang with me and Davis because Davis was getting married the next day. I suggested that we hang out at Dave & Busters and that we all could catch a movie afterwards. He told me he'll get back at me. I talked to DeAdrian to see if he wanted to hang with us. He said that his brother-in-law was having a bachelor party. I tried to find out where and if my crew could hook up and attend. He said he would find out the exact details. He called me back and said they were going to Deja Vu, a strip club. I guess we arranged that we were going to hook up. When I got home Alan was there. I called DeAdrian and he said that he was going to San Diego. I told him

Kirk wasn't going to drive that far. Kirk called me back and said that he was just going to stay home. So that left us with nowhere to go. We played cards and dominoes.

I know that it was apparent that we didn't go out. DeAdrian, okay he had plans already and I believe he was honest. Kirk, I think he just didn't want to kick it with me. The last couple of times we were supposed to kick it he FLAKED. Allison, the last few times we were supposed to kick it, FLAKED!! Davis and Latoya were supposed to come by and watch some movies with me, FLAKED!! I haven't seen Abdul in about two and a half weeks since he started working, flake! He still could find some time to come by or get in touch with me. Renee has come through for me a great deal. She was my escort to Davis's wedding even though she's in a relationship. I'm going to ask Destiny to be my escort to the next wedding that I attend. I'm in another wedding in August. I want to see if I am worth the argument with Lucas if she says she'll go with me.

I know if I was, well I don't know so I better not write what I was thinking. I paged Rebecka about 30 minutes ago, no response yet. I paged Brenda twice when I got in from work about a quarter to 8:00 p.m. She is in the neighborhood for the night. I told her I was off at 7:30 p.m. Come to find out after she left, I could have stayed an hour overtime. She didn't come up to the job and she ain't been by the crib, called, or paged me. I called Jesse, I'm pretty sure he'll call me back. Hey, he was supposed to had come out here a .... the phone rings, it's Rebecka. She said she's waiting on her mom to pick up her sister and that she would come by before 11:00 p.m. if she picks them up before then. I don't know, man, I just don't know!! Alan just stopped by to pick up his bag. He broke me off some knowledge! Now I guess I know. He told me that Jesus' friend Peter betrayed him, flaked on him (in my words). If Jesus had flakes in his life, what makes me think I won't have them in mine??

That newfound knowledge didn't stick into my fat brain for many, many years to come. I continuously sought out for solid reliable friends in vain. Disappointment after disappointment. Expectations instead of acceptance were my folly. I was alone then and I'm alone now. Teaching myself not to rely on others for sincere genuine friendships is an ongoing class for me. Learning to take people at face value is easier said than done but it is a lesson that I have to practice to master. It saddens me because I am a people person, and I love company. I think that's part of Leo in me. The Virgo part of me gets exhausted with prolonged company. Finding the balance is not easy but it is an ongoing process. Because of the corona virus and the monkey pox outbreak, the introverted Virgo in me is in overdrive. I choose not to have sexual relations of any kind at this time, be it penetration or oral. The stripper that I fucked on my birthday at the strip club in 2019 was the last time I fucked a woman. The last time I had some head and given head was with Leroy, I met him on A4A in 2013, and that was over six months ago.

The last time I actually had coitus with a man was with a dude name Marquis that I met on Grindr two years ago and I did the penetrating. Dewayne was probably the last guy to fuck me and that was approximately eight years ago. I met Dewayne on A4A. I don't feel as bad about pleasuring myself now because it is absolutely safer than ordering niggas over off of Grindr and A4A like I'm ordering a pizza. That's exactly how it is. I can go on these sites and niggas, Latinos, and even non melanin men are an order away like a fuckin pizza. Tall, short, fat, skinny, cute, handsome, big dicks, small dicks, big ass, no ass, it is all available at my beck and call. These encounters and more will be addressed in, "Now What's Next".

"When someone
shows you
who they are
believe them
the first time."
-Maya Angelou

CHAPTER VIII

Movin On

· · ◦ ● ◦ · ·

Journal insert

03SEPT2000: First things first, recognize today is my beautiful, loving, adorable daughter's Tomia's birthday!! She is blessed to see nine years on this earth. I thank God for Tomia; I truly, truly do! The situation that I am in, I just don't know. I've said it time and time again, I have so, so, so much to be grateful for. I guess because of my human desires it's just so hard for me to appreciate it. And truly, I don't think I could ever truly appreciate being separated from Tomia. I hate, and I know that's a strong word, the fact that Destiny and I couldn't or wouldn't get our SHIT together!! I HATE the fact that my so-called wife and I couldn't get our SHIT together!! I believe I truly tried. And I truly believe every time I gave her the benefit of the doubt, she FUCKED me over!! I guess her claim will always be she couldn't deal with the fact that I fucked around with men. Even though it was once with Lewis, a guy that I met at church back in 1996.

I wasn't at all attracted to him, but I figured he was gay because he was quite feminine. And time to time with Mickey. Like she was or is HOLIER than thou!! Whatever!! I'm 30 years young now and I am faced with a lot of shit, but I dare not complain because my brother, oh, my brother, I know he is faced with a great deal on his table. I don't know if I wrote about Alan's condition before but if I didn't, he's been diagnosed with Multiple Sclerosis (MS). He works two jobs and walks with a cane now. Alan was blessed with a third child on my birthday this year. She did not come out until I got to the hospital. One of the best days of my unhappy life. Maybe I have no reason to be unhappy. Maybe I have every reason to unhappy. All I know is I'm not happy.

Right now, my mom is on her way to Memphis with my uncle Ronnie. My aunt Lynn and uncle Barry are already in Memphis. You just don't know how much I want to be out there with them. Ya just don't know how much I just want to jump in my Kia Sportage and bone the FUCK OUT!!

I just came from Davis and Latoya's apartment. I had Latoya re-braid my hair because I wasn't too happy with the way Jennifer braided it. I kicked it over there for a few hours. I had bought me a bottle of Long Island Iced Tea and now I'm drinking on the rest of the beer Davis gave me. Tomorrow, Jennifer is supposed to let me use her EBT card to get Tomia a cake and ice cream for her birthday. I don't have that much cash and that's just my fault. I'm going to try to make the best of the situation. There is so much shit to write about but maybe later I'll finish.

Journal insert

07OCT2000: I'm now sitting in church waiting for the video bible class to start. I have a FEW things on my mind that are bothering me. First is my health, I'll discuss that later. Second, I just got off the phone with Keisha. Even though I filed the divorce papers last

Month, I told her I want to work things out. I had sex with her a couple of weeks ago and I was spending the night with her at her apartment. Today I called her because we've been talking lately. She told me that, "She didn't want to be with me because I let another man put his weenie in my butt and I sucked another man's weenie." (word for word). Class is starting. Hopefully I'll finish writing later.

One of the few nights that I spent with Keisha at her apartment we made love as always. Afterwards she took a shower. She came out of the bathroom wearing a robe; looking as beautiful and sweet as the day I met her. As I laid on her bed, she played a Deborah Cox CD and began to sing ....

"How did you get here? Nobody's supposed to be here
I've tried that love thing for the last time
My heart says, no, no, nobody's supposed be here
But you came along and changed my mind
I've spent all my life on a search to find
love who'll stay for eternity that heaven sent to fulfill my needs
But when I turn around, again love had not been found
heart got broke and oh it hurt so bad, I'm sad to say
love wins again
So, I place my heart under lock and key
To take some time and take care of me
Then I turn around and you're standing here
How did you get here? Nobody's supposed to be here
I've tried that love thing for the last time
My heart says, no, no, nobody's supposed to be here
But you came along and changed my mind
This time I swear I'm through but if only you knew
How many times I've said those words then fall again
When will I ever learn, do many tears I've cried
This lovely black butterfly must take the chance and
spread my wings
Love can make you do some crazy things
So, I place my heart under lock and key
To take some time and take care of me
Then I turn around and you're standing here
How did you get here?
Nobody's supposed to be here"
-Deborah Cox

I loved to hear Keisha sing. "My songbird" is what I used to call her. She had a beautiful singing voice, but when she wasn't singing to me, the things she said were cruel, hurtful, and disrespectful. Her voice was that of an angel, but the words she used during our arguments were the complete opposite. When we argued, the gloves came off, and we both hit below the belt. She hated when I called her a hood rat or ghetto—it was my go-to insult. My sexuality was always her go to.

Even though I was 28 and she was 27, we weren't mature enough to be getting married. Maybe we weren't mature enough to marry each other— or maybe just not mature enough to marry at all. I know for certain I wasn't ready. I was grappling with my sexuality. I wanted the stability of a home, someone to love me, and someone to love. But how could I truly have that when I wanted to be with men just as much as I wanted to be with women? To be with one, I'd have to deny my feelings, urges, and desires for the other. It wasn't fair—to me or to Keisha.

Yes, we got married way too fast. Absolutely, we didn't know each other well enough. And there were certainly red flags beforehand. Despite all of that, I wanted to work things out with Keisha. I wanted to work on our marriage. What that would have looked like, I honestly don't know. Could it have worked? Faith, prayer, hope—a wishing star...

A letter to Keisha from me

Unknown date

Keisha, I never ever imagined that being married would ever be this way. I wish I was stating that it was better than I have ever imagined but I'm not. It's so very true that I feel that I was pushed into this situation. But I was determined to make the best out of it. Being that you work full-time, and I work part-time, I wanted to make sure I used my extra time off to take care of the major responsibilities concerning the household chores such as: washing the laundry, folding the clothes, putting the clothes away, washing the dishes, cooking, and taking out the trash.

3L's

January 3, 2003

True enough, Life, Love, and Loneliness hurts and true
enough, it's up to the individual to make Life, Love,
and Loneliness work. Life is a gift from a Higher Being,
a true blessing.
Make peace in your life. Take time to smell the roses. Then
you'll see there is no time for stressing.
Love, love is something that should never ever be
taken advantage of.
Love is truly a precious sincere gift from the
Higher Being above.

Loneliness is a temporary state. A time in our lives when we must recognize, realize, and analyze who we truly are as an individual and strive to go on and carry on and to be strong. Because after all, upon this earth God did not intend for man to be alone.

-Ignatius J

June 29, 2006

"You cannot live life
in cruise control
sometimes you have to
move a little faster
or move a little slower"

-Ignatius J

The last time I had any type of communication with Keisha was about 15 years ago through a post I made on my Facebook page that she responded to. A few things that I admired about Mrs. Thomas: She was seriously committed to her education which made her book smart. Working in the education system was her go-to and strong point. Keisha was beautiful and had a very beautiful singing voice. She remarried in 2022, and I believe she is still living in Las Vegas. I wish her nothing but love, peace, and a happy healthy life.

The Continuation of: *Two Baby Mama's, an ExWife, and an Ex–Boyfriend, Now What's Next??*

The Second Baby Mama and the Ex-Boyfriend

Now What's Next??

I'm in the Army Now!! February of 2001, I joined the United States Army. I put in a two week notice at Smart and Final after eight years! It was a great job filled with so many great memories. Forever grateful and appreciative for all that it was to me. I still have dreams about being there working. Getting into the Army was very challenging for me. The alcohol intake wasn't my issue. The exigent demands of cutting out smoking weed to join was my issue. My recruiter Sgt. Monday was very patient and understanding with me. He advised me to, "Just stop smoking for two weeks and it'll be out of your system and then you'll be able to get you in."

This was after he took me to an offsite location to get tested for marijuana and I failed. He even went as far as getting me something to drink to clean my system. A lot of options were in front of me as far as where I wanted to be stationed and what job (MOS) I wanted. Being stationed in Germany and being a Chaplin Assistant was heavy on my mind. But nooooo my ass chose to go to Korea and be a cook. My main thought was my friend Mark from Smart and Final. He was stationed in South Korea and someday I want to own my own restaurant. No regrets, no regrets. Everything happens for a reason.

Naomi Charmaine Pain AKA Pvt. Pain

-The Second Baby Mama

I met Naomi when I got stationed at Fort Lewis, Washington in November of 2002. We were in the same unit. Tall, dark skin complexion, fine, and a walk that was captivating and sexy as hell to me. Her smile, lips, teeth, and body were all on POINT! She was a fellow soldier, an E3 Private First Class, and I was an E5 Specialist. Naomi was dating a sergeant so trying to get at her wasn't on my mind. Besides, I had just arrived at Fort Lewis that October. My attention was still slightly on having Destiny move up to Washington from California with Tomia and Precious (my goddaughter) and we would get housing. I told Destiny if she moved to Washington, she would not have to worry about anything and that I would take care of everything as far as bills; the rent would be taken care of by the military. That offer laid on her lap until it became null and void SMDH!! As she continued to be unsure and reluctant I continued to move onward.

"I'm tired of broken street glass.
Not gettin' no ass unless the
babies sleep.
But even then, it seems like
we're tryin' to keep.
Tired of payin' taxes, sendin'
me mails and faxes.
Tired of black folk complain
that crime don't stop.
I want to go to a place
where lovers go."
-Kindred the Family

My mom passed May 6th, 2006. Destiny arrived in New York with our daughter Tomia and with her daughter Precious (my goddaughter). A day or two after Destiny's arrival, Renee landed in the Big Apple. Of course, Destiny hated that. She was still holding a grudge against Renee, and she made sure I knew it. Me being in mourning did not mean shit. I was really appreciative that Destiny and Renee came. Destiny and the girls stayed in my mother's apartment with me. Renee stayed with my aunt Darlene over in the Bronx. Nothing sexual happened with either of them. Their support and being there were what I needed mentally. Renee even bought my mom's dress that she wore for the services; a red one which was her favorite color.

Stairway to Heaven
"Here we go
Climbing the stairway to heaven
Here we go
Walking the road of ecstasy
Taking the load
Of this whole world off our
shoulders
The door is wide open for you
The door is open for me
Here we go
Still in a moment of pleasure
You and I
We are gonna find the pirates
treasure
Here we go
Oh Mama, here we go
Climbing the stairway to heaven
Climbing the stairway to heaven
And we are going step by step
Together, step by step."
-The O'Jays/ Ignatius J

Memphis once again became my home in October of 2006. I drove twenty-two hours straight with my uncle Ronnie riding shot gun from New York in my Ford Explorer. My aunt Darlene did not want me to drive by myself and insisted that uncle Ronnie ride with me. I guess that was a good thing because I was planning on stopping and getting a hotel and finding some "company". The passing of my mother broke me in half. The bittersweet of it was being able to share the last year of her life with her. There were no signs of any type of illness. She had a heart attack right in front of me and suddenly died. I was absolutely DEVASTATED!! When my mother passed, I moved in with my Aunt Darlene in the Bronx. I had just gotten promoted to Customer Service Supervisor at the Old Navy on 125th Street in Harlem. I didn't want to be in New York anymore and decided to transfer and move back to Memphis.

Jackie (Same Jackie from childhood) and I came to an arranged agreement that I would rent a room from her. The first red flag was that she didn't have a room set up for me when I arrived. The second red flag was she doubled my rent the very next month!!! SMDH!! I moved into my cousin Summer's townhouse. She was supposedly Uncle Ronnie's daughter but there was never a DNA done to prove it. Summer had a four-bedroom townhouse and only her mother stayed there. She was cool on the rent, and I had all the freedom I wanted and I could smoke inside. All I did was go to work, come home and drink, go find something to eat and go to bed. Waking up just about every night crying and bawling my eyes out became a norm. I talked to no one. I mourned alone with alcohol. By this time, I was deep down the rabbit hole with the hole closing up all around me.

Raphael Romeo

-The Ex-Boyfriend

On one of my many, many drunken nights in search of food, I decided on McDonald's. Driving drunk became an every night thing for me. I was extremely depressed and overwhelmed with grief. I drove up to the McDonald's drive thru around the corner from where I was staying on an April night in 2007. The voice of the cashier through the drive thru microphone was that of a male but I can tell he had "sugar in his tank" lol but frfr. I ordered a Filet o Fish meal. When I drove up to the window to pay and pick up my food, I saw whom I had ordered from. Indeed, a male, cute, caramel complexion, hair in a pony tail with a lil sweetness in his voice. Before he handed me my food, I requested that he put his number in the bag with my food. He did so and that is when I met Raphael Romeo.

"I can say with great certainty
and absolute honesty
that I did not know what love was
until I knew
what love was not."
-P. T. Berkey

"You got me trippin, stumbling,
Flippin, fumbling
Clumsy cuz I'm fallin in love
You got me slippin, tumbling,
Sinking, fumbling,
Clumsy cuz I'm fallin in love
So in love with you."
-Fergie